AVOY PUBLISHING
· The Complete Estate & Property Planning Series ·
· Book 4 of 4 ·

ESTATE TAXES EXPLAINED

◆

A Clear Guide to Understanding Tax Impact and Preserving Wealth

A. Perkins
AVOY PUBLISHING
First Edition · 2026

Estate Taxes Explained: A Clear Guide to Understanding Tax Impact and Preserving Wealth.

First Edition · 2026 · Printed in the United States of America.

Published in the United States of America by AVOY, LLC ('AVOY Publishing'). AVOY, LLC maintains the worldwide publication and distribution rights to this work.

Permissions and editorial inquiries may be directed to ap@avoyhq.com.

Print ISBN (Hardcover): 978-1-969048-91-3

Print ISBN (Paperback): 978-1-969048-90-6

eBook ISBN: 978-1-969048-92-0

Audiobook ISBN: 978-1-969048-93-7

Cover design and interior typography by AVOY, LLC. Typeset in Georgia and presented in the AVOY house style: burgundy and bronze on cream.

Publisher's Cataloging-in-Publication data available upon request.

For the families who fear the tax

more than the loss,

and for the planners who explain the difference

between what is owed and what is feared.

Estate taxes are not universal.

They are not arbitrary.

They do not apply simply because someone died.

They apply when specific conditions are met.

Estate Taxes Explained

LEGAL NOTICE & DISCLAIMER

◆

This book is intended for general educational and informational purposes only. It does not constitute, and is not a substitute for, legal, tax, accounting, investment, insurance, or other professional advice. The federal and state transfer-tax regimes — estate tax, gift tax, generation-skipping transfer tax, income-tax basis rules, and the related procedural requirements — are governed by the Internal Revenue Code, by Treasury regulations, by case law, and by the individual states; statutes, exemption amounts, rate schedules, and procedural rules vary materially by jurisdiction and change over time. Application of any concept discussed in these pages to a particular set of facts requires individualized counsel from a qualified, licensed professional admitted to practice in the relevant jurisdiction.

Specific dollar figures, exemption thresholds, rate schedules, and indexing adjustments are stated as in effect at the time of writing and will change. The federal estate-tax exemption in particular is subject to scheduled and unscheduled statutory changes; readers must obtain current figures before acting. Discussion of state estate, inheritance, gift, and income-tax provisions — including the regimes of California, Florida, Texas, New York, Nevada, Pennsylvania, Illinois, and selected other jurisdictions — is offered at a conceptual and comparative level. Such discussion is neither exhaustive nor a substitute for the underlying statutes and regulations, which should be consulted directly together with current case law and ruling guidance.

Names, fact patterns, and dialogue used in case studies, hypothetical examples, and "What This Looks Like in Practice" sections are illustrative composites. Any resemblance to actual persons, families, decedents, executors, trustees, beneficiaries, or estates is coincidental and unintentional. No client-attorney, client-CPA, or advisor-client relationship is formed by reading this book or by following any example within it.

Discussion of tax-planning strategies, including the use of trusts, lifetime gifts, valuation discounts, generation-skipping transfers, charitable structures, and basis-step-up techniques, is for educational context only. Any actual implementation requires professional analysis of the specific family circumstances, asset composition, and applicable federal and state law. Strategies described in general terms in this volume may produce sharply different outcomes for different families and may be inappropriate or unavailable for some.

Neither the author nor AVOY, LLC, nor any contributor, editor, or reviewer accepts liability for any loss or damage caused, directly or indirectly, by reliance on the contents of this book. Readers are urged to obtain individualized professional advice before making any transfer, gift, election, filing, valuation, or planning decision that may have tax consequences.

By continuing to read this book, the reader acknowledges and accepts the terms of this notice.

CONTENTS

◆

A LETTER FROM THE PUBLISHER

◆

"Estate planning is not paperwork. It is the form love takes when it has to outlast the person who felt it."

Estate Taxes Explained begins with a quiet truth most families never say out loud: the reason we don't talk about what happens after we're gone is that we love the people we'd be talking to. Avoidance feels like protection. This book gently reframes that instinct. It shows that estate planning is not paperwork and not a confession of mortality — it is, as the epigraph above puts it, the form love takes when it has to outlast the person who felt it. Read in that spirit, every chapter becomes less about tax law and more about the daughter who won't have to scramble through unfamiliar paperwork in the worst week of her life, the spouse who will keep the house instead of being forced to sell it, and the family business that gets passed down whole rather than dismantled to satisfy a deadline.

The emotional throughline of these pages is reassurance held in tension with urgency. Reassurance, because the great majority of American families will owe no federal estate tax at all; the dread is almost always larger than the exposure.

Urgency, because the surprises that do strike — life insurance that's quietly counted, retained interests that defeat a gift, a state threshold a tenth the size of the federal one, a basis step-up forfeited by sloppy titling — are almost never caused by missing rules. They are caused by structures that were never put in place, by conversations that were never had, by a single Form 706 election that was never filed because no one realized it could double a couple's exemption. This book closes on the conviction that drives the whole AVOY series: the structures exist, the rules are knowable, and the cure for almost every estate-tax surprise is engagement during the years when engagement still matters. The goal is not to leave behind a tax-optimized estate. It is to leave behind a family that feels chosen, prepared, and loved on the far side of grief.

If you have opened this book, you are almost certainly one of three kinds of reader.

You may be someone who has heard, somewhere along the way, that estate taxes are about to take half of what you spent your life building. The phrase has lodged itself in your mind. You have not been able to shake it. You have come to this book because you want, finally, to know whether the fear is justified — and what, if anything, to do about it.

You may be someone who has just become responsible for an estate that exceeds what you had thought of as the threshold. The estate-planning attorney has used phrases like Form 706 and applicable exclusion amount and portability election. The CPA has mentioned alternate valuation dates and generation-skipping inclusion. You have nodded politely and are now trying to learn, in private, what those phrases actually mean and what the consequences of getting them wrong might be.

Or you may be someone who has heard, more recently, that estate taxes do not apply to most American families. The relief was real. But you have begun to suspect that the story is more complicated than that — that there are state-level taxes you may not have considered, that there are basis questions that matter even when there is no estate tax, that there are timing rules that catch families off guard. You want, just once, for someone to tell you the whole picture in plain language.

This book is for all three of you.

Estate Taxes Explained is Book 4 of The Complete Estate & Property Planning Series — the four-volume institutional reference comprising Trust Made Simple (Book 1), Probate Explained (Book 2), Property After Death (Book 3), and Estate Taxes Explained (Book 4, this volume). The series, taken together, treats the four pillars of American post-mortem asset transfer. This volume completes the set by treating the tax overlay that shapes the entire structure for substantial estates — and that, even for estates well below the federal threshold, frequently shapes outcomes through state-level regimes, gift-tax interactions, and the fundamental income-tax rules that govern basis at death.

The book takes a position. It says that estate taxes generate more fear than they deserve and produce more surprise than they should. The fear comes from misunderstanding when the tax applies. The surprise comes from misunderstanding what gets counted. Once those two questions are settled honestly, most of the anxiety drops away — and what remains is a tractable planning problem that has well-developed answers.

"Most American estates do not pay federal estate tax. Those that do tend to be surprised not by the tax itself, but by what was included."

We have written it on the assumption that you are an intelligent adult who has been talked down to enough times by people in suits. Where the tax law is technical, we say so. Where it is not, we use ordinary words. Where the outcome depends on a state-by-state distinction — the surprising number of states that have their own estate tax with much lower thresholds, the fewer states with inheritance taxes, the community-property states where basis treatment is sharply more favorable — we point that out and tell you which states fall on which side of the line.

Particular care has been taken with the moments when families consistently get caught: the discovery that a life-insurance policy the deceased thought was outside the estate is fully included for tax purposes; the realization that a state-level estate tax with a two-million-dollar threshold applies even though the federal exemption is twenty times higher; the surprise that lifetime gifts made years before death still affect the estate-tax calculation; the discovery that a trust the deceased treated as a planning achievement is fully includible because the deceased retained a particular power. Each of these moments has its own logic. Each has its own way of producing avoidable expense and avoidable distress. We will spend time on all of them.

We are not your tax counsel. The Legal Notice on the previous page is not ceremonial. The transfer-tax system sits at the intersection of the Internal Revenue Code, fifty state regimes, and the lived realities of families that are usually meeting these rules for the first time. A book can show you the architecture. It cannot file your Form 706 or compute your particular generation-skipping inclusion. When you act on something in these pages, do it with the help of qualified counsel and a CPA in the relevant jurisdiction.

With that, we offer you the volume.

— AVOY Publishing

Spring 2026

HOW TO READ THIS BOOK

◆

The book is organized in six movements.

You can read them in order, the way they were written, and you will end up with a complete mental model of the American transfer-tax system: what it is, when it applies, what it counts, why timing matters more than amounts, how it interacts with the income-tax basis rules, and how to think about the planning that minimizes it. By the time you reach the Conclusion you will know more about estate taxes than ninety-five percent of the population — including most executors and most beneficiaries who arrive at their first meeting with the estate's CPA.

Or you can read whichever Part answers the question you came with. Each chapter stands alone. The cross-references will get you back to anything you skipped.

A few suggestions, depending on who you are.

If you are afraid of estate taxes and want to know whether the fear is justified.

Read Chapter 1 first (what estate taxes actually are), then Chapter 5 (the exemption system), then Chapter 10 (why people get surprised). Those three chapters together will tell you, with reasonable confidence, whether your particular family will face a federal estate-tax exposure. For most readers the answer is no, and the remaining chapters become reference material.

If you are administering an estate that has tax exposure now.

Read Chapter 4 (what gets counted in the gross estate) carefully. Then Chapter 6 (timing and the date-of-death valuation) and Chapter 7 (gift-tax interactions). Those three chapters cover the computational backbone of any actual estate-tax filing.

If you are planning during life and want to understand the basis-step-up.

Read Chapters 8 and 9 first. The basis-step-up at death is, for many American families, a more financially significant rule than the estate tax itself — and the planning interactions between basis and estate tax are the single most consequential planning area for families with appreciated property.

If you are dealing with a state-level estate or inheritance tax.
Read Chapter 2 (the difference between estate and inheritance tax). Then read Chapter 5 with attention to the state-level discussion. Twelve states and the District of Columbia maintain estate taxes with thresholds well below the federal exemption; six maintain inheritance taxes. State exposure is real for many families who have no federal exposure.

A note on the prose. Where the book uses a technical term — applicable exclusion amount, deceased spousal unused exclusion, generation-skipping transfer, qualified terminable interest property, alternate valuation date, basis carryover — the term is defined the first time it appears, and re-defined any time it shows up in a chapter where the reader may have lost the thread. Where the law is truly complicated, we say so and slow down. Where it is not, we move quickly. The Glossary in the back catches anything that drifts.

A Note on the Reading Conventions

Three small visual conventions appear throughout the book. They are easy to recognize and worth understanding before you begin.

Chapter at a Glance

Every chapter opens with a short bullet list under the heading "Chapter at a Glance." It tells you what the chapter is about and what you will know by the end. Read it as a map. Skip it if you would rather discover the territory as you go.

KEY POINT callouts

Boxed in burgundy with a "KEY POINT" label, these are the most important structural facts in each chapter. If you are skim-reading, read the KEY POINT boxes.

REFLECTION callouts

Boxed in bronze with a "REFLECTION" label, these are quieter notes — observations about how the tax intersects with families and with the deeper question of what the transfer-tax system is for. Skip them if you are reading in a hurry; return to them later when the work is closer.

WHEN DOES ESTATE TAX APPLY? definition box

Boxed in steel-blue and labeled "WHEN DOES ESTATE TAX APPLY?", this single callout appears in the Preface and supplies the working answer to the question that drives the entire book. If you read nothing else before Chapter 1, read that box.

What This Looks Like in Practice

Most chapters include a short narrative vignette under this heading. The vignettes are illustrative composites — names and details are invented, but the patterns they describe are common in tax practice. They are intended to ground the abstract architecture of the chapter in the texture of a real family's experience.

Tables, Figures, and the Glossary

Tables are labeled "Table X.X" and figures are labeled "Figure X.X." They are integrated into the text where they help, never as decoration. The Glossary in the back of the book defines every technical term used in the chapters; if a word stops you, the Glossary will start you again.

What's at the Back of This Book

Roughly the back third of this volume is reference material. It is meant to be returned to long after the first reading. We list it here so you know what is waiting for you when you need it.

- **Conclusion.** The philosophical close — what the transfer-tax system is for, in plain language.
- **Reader FAQ.** Common questions, organized by category — Federal Estate & Gift Tax, State Tax Regimes, and Basis & Capital Gains — with every answer cross-referenced to the chapter that treats it in full.
- **Glossary of Tax Terms.** More than fifty entries. Every technical word in the book, defined in plain English, with chapter cross-references.
- **Bibliography & Reference Guide.** Statutory sources, treatises, practitioner guides, IRS publications, and online resources for the reader who wants to dig deeper.
- **About the Publisher and About the Author.** AVOY Publishing's mission and the author's background.

- **Fourteen Appendices (A–N).** Tax at a Glance · State Estate & Inheritance Tax Map · The Form 706 Filing Checklist · Common Tax Forms and What They Mean · Sample Letter to Heirs Regarding Tax Matters · Annotated Reading List · Twelve-Month Estate-Tax Calendar · Family Tax Communication Framework · Subject Index · Reader's Quick-Start Guide · Notes on The Complete Estate & Property Planning Series · Chapter-by-Chapter Summary · Generation-Skipping Transfer Reference · Charitable Planning Structures.

Together the back matter is a compact reference library. If you came to the book because of an immediate filing question, the Reader's Quick-Start Guide (Appendix J) and the Form 706 Filing Checklist (Appendix C) will be the most useful pages you read this week.

Begin where it serves you. Return as your circumstances change. The book is designed for both first reading and tenth.

A NOTE ON THE MAKING OF THIS VOLUME

◆

A book like this could be written in two ways.

It could be written by a transfer-tax specialist, in the language transfer-tax specialists use, with a reference to a Treasury regulation on every other page and a chapter on the Chapter 14 valuation rules that nobody outside the field finishes. Several such books exist. They are useful to specialists.

Or it could be written by someone who has watched the transfer-tax system unfold from the other side of the kitchen table — who has sat with families during the months after a death while the CPA explained the inclusion calculation, watched executors discover that the life insurance they had treated as separate was fully includible, watched first-time filers grapple with the alternate valuation election, and listened to the same misunderstandings repeat themselves across a hundred different families. That is the perspective from which this book is written.

The author is not a tax attorney or a CPA, and does not pretend to be one. He is, however, someone who has spent more than a decade observing private estate administration in close proximity — as an executor, as a trustee, as a settlor of structures that have produced their own filing requirements, and as the person whom families in his orbit have turned to when they did not know who else to ask. The result is a book that takes the tax law seriously without pretending to be the tax law itself.

Where the text describes a federal exemption amount, a state threshold, or a procedural rule, the description is grounded in the rule as it stood at the time of writing. Where the text describes how the system performs in real life, the description is grounded in observation of how it has performed for real families over the past decade and longer.

This is, in short, a practitioner's book — written for readers who would rather understand the architecture than be sold a brochure of it.

PREFACE

◆

The first thing to know about estate taxes is that they generate more fear than almost any other part of estate administration.

People hear large numbers. They hear phrases like death tax. They hear conflicting explanations from friends, advisors, headlines, and political campaigns. They are told, by various people with various agendas, that the tax will take half of everything; that the tax barely applies anymore; that the tax is about to be repealed; that the tax is about to be expanded. None of these statements is fully true. None is fully false. The truth lives in the spaces between them, and almost nobody explains it cleanly.

> **WHEN DOES ESTATE TAX APPLY?**
>
> WHEN DOES ESTATE TAX APPLY? Federal estate tax applies when a deceased person's gross estate, plus the value of certain lifetime gifts, exceeds the applicable exclusion amount in effect at death. State estate taxes apply when a deceased resident's estate exceeds the applicable state threshold. Inheritance taxes apply, in six states, to particular categories of beneficiary regardless of estate size. Most American estates pay none of these. The estates that pay are surprised — almost without exception — by what specifically was included rather than by the existence of the tax itself.

Most of the fear comes from not understanding when estate taxes actually apply — and when they do not. This book exists to explain the system, not as a threat, but as a structured set of rules that produce predictable outcomes once the rules are understood.

Estate taxes are not universal. They are not arbitrary. They do not apply simply because someone died. They apply when specific conditions are met. Once those conditions are understood, the fear drops away and the surprises largely disappear.

The transfer-tax system is also not just one tax. It is a coordinated set of three related taxes — estate tax, gift tax, and generation-skipping transfer tax — plus a separate income-tax provision (the basis-step-up under Internal Revenue Code section 1014) that, for many families, matters more financially than any of the transfer taxes themselves. Understanding the system means understanding how these four pieces interact. Most of the surprises families experience come from focusing on one of the four and missing the others.

We will move through the system in stages. We will begin with what estate taxes are and what they are not. We will move into the structural distinction between estate tax and inheritance tax — a distinction that confuses families and produces real expense when it is missed. We will spend the middle of the book on the gross estate (what gets counted), the exemption system (why it usually rescues most families), and the timing rules (why timing matters more than amounts). We will turn in

Part IV to the gift-tax interaction. Part V will treat the basis-step-up and capital gains, the income-tax provisions that govern what happens when inherited property is eventually sold. We will close in Part VI with the question of why families get surprised by estate taxes — and how the patterns of surprise are almost all preventable with appropriate planning during life.

Read with patience. The subject rewards it.

INTRODUCTION

Why This Book Exists

◆

Estate taxes generate more fear than almost any other part of estate administration.

People hear large numbers. They hear phrases like death tax. They hear conflicting explanations from friends, advisors, and headlines.

Most of that fear comes from not understanding when estate taxes actually apply — and when they do not.

This book exists to explain estate taxes as a system, not as a threat. Estate taxes are not universal. They are not arbitrary. They do not apply simply because someone died. They apply when specific conditions are met. Once those conditions are understood, the fear drops away and the surprises largely disappear.

Most American estates pay no federal estate tax. The current federal applicable exclusion amount — the threshold below which no federal estate tax applies — is, at the time of writing, in the millions of dollars per individual and approximately twice that for married couples using portability. Roughly 0.1 percent of American deaths produce a federal estate-tax filing obligation, and an even smaller fraction produce actual tax. For the great majority of families, the federal estate tax is a non-event.

But the federal estate tax is not the whole story. Twelve states and the District of Columbia maintain their own estate taxes, with exemption thresholds typically a fraction of the federal level — sometimes as low as one or two million dollars. Six states maintain inheritance taxes, which apply to specific categories of beneficiary regardless of the estate's size. The federal gift-tax system runs in parallel and uses the same exemption pool. The federal generation-skipping transfer tax applies to transfers that skip a generation. And the income-tax basis-step-up rules, which determine the tax owed when inherited property is eventually sold, can be more financially significant than any of the transfer taxes themselves.

This book exists for one reason: to explain the entire transfer-tax system as it actually operates — without fear, without salesmanship, and without pretending it is simpler than it is. Estate planning is not paperwork and not a confession of mortality. It is the form love takes when it has to outlast the person who felt it. Every rule explained in these pages exists to serve that purpose, or to be navigated so that it does not defeat it.

Estate taxes are not punishment.

They are not random.

They are not always avoidable.

They are a coordinated set of statutory rules that apply when specific conditions are met.

Once you understand the structure, much of the anxiety drops away — and what remains is a planning problem with well-developed answers.

Every year, a number of American families lose meaningful value to four particular categories of tax surprise.

The first is included assets — the discovery that something the family treated as outside the taxable estate (a life-insurance policy held by the deceased, a property the deceased gifted but retained the right to occupy, a trust the deceased could amend) is fully includible for tax purposes. Inclusion is a more consequential question than exemption, because inclusion is applied first.

The second is state-level tax — the surprise that a family comfortably below the federal exemption is materially exposed at the state level. State thresholds in Massachusetts, Oregon, and Washington (among others) are sharply lower than the federal exemption, and many families discover this only after the death.

The third is timing — the realization that lifetime gifts made years before death still count in the estate-tax calculation, or that valuation dates fix tax exposure at moments the family did not anticipate.

The fourth is basis — the discovery that the income-tax consequences of how an asset is inherited (with full step-up, with no step-up, with carryover basis) often dominate the transfer-tax consequences for the family that eventually sells the asset. Basis is the most important tax provision most families have never heard of.

Each of these four exposures can be planned for. Some can be eliminated entirely with the right structures put in place during life. Most can be sharply reduced even when the structure is already set.

This book exists because most of what is written about estate taxes is written either for tax specialists — and is therefore unreadable to anyone else — or for marketing purposes, and is therefore not telling the whole truth. The space in the middle — a book that respects the reader's intelligence, defines its terms, takes the tax law seriously, names what each part of the system does and does not do, and tells the truth about the practical experience of actually facing the tax — has been mostly empty.

We wrote this volume to fill it.

By the time you finish, you will know:

- What estate taxes are, structurally, and what they are not.
- The difference between estate tax and inheritance tax, and which states have which.
- Why the transfer-tax system exists, in plain language.

- What gets counted in the gross estate — and why this is the question that produces most of the surprise.
- How the federal exemption works, why it has changed, and why the state thresholds matter at least as much.
- Why timing matters more than amounts, and how to think about valuation and the date-of-death rule.
- How gift taxes connect to estate taxes through the unified credit and the lifetime-exemption pool.
- What basis is, why the step-up at death is one of the most important rules in American tax law, and how it applies to different forms of ownership.
- How capital-gains tax interacts with estate tax — and why understanding that interaction often matters more than understanding either tax in isolation.
- Why families get surprised by estate taxes, and the specific patterns that produce most of the surprises.

This is not legal advice. It is not tax advice. It is a foundation. With it, you will be in a position to ask better questions, evaluate better answers, and make better decisions about a system that arrives, sooner or later, in many American families that have built something worth passing on.

That is the value of a book like this.

Let us begin.

PART I

FOUNDATIONS

What estate taxes are, what they are not, and the structural distinction that confuses most families.

CHAPTER 1

What Estate Taxes Are — and What They Are Not

Chapter at a Glance

- What estate taxes actually are — taxes on the transfer of wealth at death, imposed on the estate.
- What estate taxes are not — income tax, inheritance tax, automatic, or universal.
- Why beneficiaries do not personally owe federal estate tax.
- The categorical separation between estate tax, gift tax, GST, income tax, and capital-gains tax.
- How to read Table 1.1 — the eight common transfer-related taxes families confuse.

Estate taxes are taxes on the transfer of wealth at death.

That sentence sounds simple. The simplicity hides three distinctions that families consistently miss, and missing them is the single most common source of estate-tax confusion in ordinary practice. Before we can talk about exemptions, thresholds, exclusions, or planning structures, the categorical differences have to be settled clearly.

Estate taxes are not:

- taxes on income
- taxes on inheritances (in most states)
- taxes on beneficiaries receiving money
- taxes that apply automatically to every estate
- taxes that take half of everything, despite what marketing literature has long suggested

Estate taxes are assessed against the estate itself, not against individual heirs. This distinction matters more than it sounds like it should.

The Estate as Taxpayer

When a person dies, the law treats the estate as a separate taxpayer for federal income-tax purposes for the duration of the administration. The estate gets its own employer identification number. It files its own annual income-tax return (Form 1041) on any income earned during administration. And, where the gross estate exceeds the federal threshold, it files a one-time transfer-tax return (Form 706) reporting the value of the deceased's transferable wealth and computing whatever estate tax is owed.

The estate's executor or personal representative is responsible for filing these returns and for paying any tax due. The tax is paid from estate assets before any distribution to beneficiaries.

Beneficiaries do not personally owe federal estate tax. They receive whatever is left after the estate has satisfied its obligations — and from the federal estate-tax perspective, the receipt itself is not a taxable event for them.

This is a critical point. Beneficiaries often assume they personally owe the tax. They almost always do not, at least for federal estate-tax purposes. The estate handles the obligation before anything reaches them.

> **KEY POINT**
>
> Federal estate tax is paid by the estate, not by the beneficiaries who eventually receive the property. The tax is satisfied from estate assets before distribution. Beneficiaries take what is left, free of further federal estate-tax liability on the same property.

What Estate Tax Is Not — In More Detail

Three confusions deserve specific treatment because each produces real planning errors when it is not corrected early.

(1) Estate tax is not income tax. The federal estate tax under Internal Revenue Code Chapter 11 is an excise on the privilege of transferring property at death. It is computed on the value of the gross estate (with deductions and exemptions), not on income generated by that property. The income-tax consequences of inheriting property are separate questions, governed by different sections of the Code, and we treat them in Chapters 8 and 9. Confusing the two leads to misanalysis:

families sometimes plan to avoid estate tax in ways that increase income tax, or vice versa, and the loss can be material.

(2) Estate tax is not inheritance tax. Estate tax is imposed on the estate of the deceased; inheritance tax is imposed on the beneficiary who receives property. The federal government does not impose an inheritance tax. Six states do. The terminology matters because the planning is sharply different — a strategy that minimizes estate tax may not affect inheritance tax at all. We treat the distinction in Chapter 2.

(3) Estate tax is not a tax on death. It is a tax on the transfer of wealth at death. The distinction matters because it explains why some transfers occurring at death are taxable and others are not — assets passing to a surviving spouse, for example, qualify for the unlimited marital deduction and pass estate-tax-free regardless of value, while the same assets passing to anyone else are fully includible. The tax is concerned with the transfer event, not the death event.

What Estate Tax Is, Then

Estate tax is a federal excise — and in some states, an additional state-level excise — imposed on the transfer of a deceased person's wealth, computed on the gross estate after applicable deductions and reduced by the applicable exclusion amount. It is paid by the estate. It applies only when the estate exceeds specified thresholds. Most American estates pay no estate tax.

Table 1.1

Tax	Imposed on	When
Federal estate tax	The estate (transferable wealth)	Once, at death, if gross estate exceeds federal exclusion.
Federal gift tax	The donor (lifetime transfers)	When lifetime transfers exceed annual exclusions and use lifetime credit.
Federal generation-skipping transfer tax	Transfers skipping a generation	On gifts/bequests to grandchildren or further-removed beneficiaries.
Federal income tax (estate's Form 1041)	Income earned by the estate during administration	Annually until the estate closes.
State estate tax (12 states + DC)	The estate (transferable wealth)	Once, at death, if gross estate exceeds state threshold.
State inheritance tax (6 states)	The beneficiary	When a beneficiary receives an inheritance from a state resident.
Capital-gains tax (after sale)	The seller	When inherited property is later sold at a gain over basis.
Property tax (state/local)	The owner of real property	Annually, regardless of any death event.

Estate tax versus other taxes families confuse it with.

Table 1.1 is worth memorizing in rough form. Most of the questions that arise in actual estate-tax administration trace back to clarifying which row of the table the family is in. When the executor's CPA mentions a generation-skipping tax, they mean the third row, not the first. When a beneficiary asks whether they will owe tax on what they receive, they are usually asking about the second-to-last row (or, where applicable, the inheritance-tax row).

Why This Distinction Matters

It is worth pausing on why the categorical separation matters in practice, beyond simple definitional cleanliness.

Beneficiaries who think they personally owe estate tax often make decisions on that incorrect assumption — declining to accept inheritances they could have safely accepted, structuring receipts in needlessly complex ways, paying tax-preparation fees for filings they did not need to make. None of this is necessary in the federal system. The tax is owed by the estate, paid by the estate, and beneficiaries' federal-estate-tax exposure is structurally limited.

Conversely, beneficiaries in states with inheritance taxes sometimes assume the federal-system rule applies — that the estate handles all tax — and discover only after the fact that they owe a state inheritance tax personally on what they received. The six states with inheritance taxes do not work the same way, and the difference is real money for affected beneficiaries.

The categorical separation is the foundation. We will spend the rest of the book building structures on top of it.

What This Looks Like in Practice

A widow — call her Helen — receives notice that she is the sole beneficiary of her late husband's $3 million estate. She has heard, somewhere, that estate taxes can consume large portions of estates. She is concerned. She calls her CPA in panic.

The CPA explains, over a single fifteen-minute call, that Helen owes nothing in federal estate tax. Three structural facts dispose of her concern: first, her husband's estate is well below the federal exemption and would owe no federal tax even if she were not the spouse. Second, even if there had been federal tax exposure, she would not personally owe the tax — the estate would. Third, transfers to her as the surviving spouse qualify for the unlimited marital deduction; no federal estate tax applies on transfers to her regardless of estate size. Helen is in three layers of structural protection from the tax she had been fearing.

The fifteen minutes saves Helen weeks of needless worry. The savings was structural — understanding what the tax is, who pays it, and what the marital deduction does. Most calls of this kind end the same way.

Where We Go From Here

Notes on Practice

Two practical patterns are worth flagging here. First, the most consistent observation in tax practice is that fear of estate tax is disproportionate to actual exposure. Most families who arrive at an estate-planning appointment worried about estate tax discover, often within the first hour, that they have no federal exposure at all. The relief is real. The fear was real. The two were never well-correlated.

Second, the categorical confusion between estate tax, inheritance tax, and capital-gains tax persists despite being addressable with a fifteen-minute explanation. Counsel and CPAs should be willing to have the categorical conversation early, before any specific planning discussion. Without the categorical foundation, more advanced discussions tend to drift into confusion.

Practitioner Patterns — Beyond the Categories

Three additional patterns about the categorical structure are worth recording for the careful practitioner.

First, the income-tax-and-estate-tax interaction at the level of the estate's administrative operations. An estate generates ordinary income during administration — interest, dividends, rental income, trust income — that is reported on the estate's Form 1041, separate from the one-time Form 706. Tax elections on the 1041 (deductibility of administrative expenses against income vs. against estate-tax base) require attention. Most CPA error in estate-tax practice arises from sloppy interaction between the two regimes. The estate's executor and CPA must decide explicitly, in each year, where to claim each deductible expense. The 706 deduction reduces estate tax at potentially 40% rates; the 1041 deduction reduces ordinary income at the estate's marginal rate (often higher in compressed trust brackets). The optimization is fact-specific, but the decision should be made deliberately.

Second, the deceased's final personal income-tax return (Form 1040 for the year of death). This return covers the deceased's income from January 1 through the date of death. It is filed by the executor and is an income-tax return separate from both the estate's 1041 and the estate's 706. Three filings, three different bases of computation, three different deadlines. Each captures a different slice of tax life. Coordination across the three is one of the things estate-specialist CPAs do that general-practice accountants sometimes do not.

Third, the categorical separation between federal and state. State estate taxes follow their own rules; state inheritance taxes follow their own rules; some states have decoupled from federal rules over time so that a federal exemption increase does not affect state thresholds. Counsel should not assume federal rules tell the state story. Massachusetts and Oregon in particular have decoupled fully from federal in recent decades; New York maintains a partially decoupled system; Connecticut and Maine have re-coupled to federal. Each move has changed planning meaningfully for residents of the affected states.

Edge Case — The Non-Citizen Spouse

An important variation on the marital-deduction rule deserves explicit treatment because it traps families with international ties. The unlimited marital deduction under IRC §2056 applies only to transfers to a US citizen surviving spouse. Transfers to a non-citizen surviving spouse do not qualify for the unlimited deduction. The cure is the qualified domestic trust (QDOT) under IRC §2056A — a specialized trust structure designed to allow effectively-deferred federal estate tax on transfers to non-citizen spouses, with rules ensuring the tax is eventually paid when distributions are made or the surviving spouse dies.

The QDOT must satisfy specific requirements: at least one trustee must be a US citizen or domestic corporation; the trustee must withhold estate tax on certain distributions of principal; the trust must hold assets sufficient to satisfy the deferred tax. Counsel handling estates with non-citizen spouses should engage the QDOT analysis specifically. The structure works but requires deliberate implementation and ongoing administration.

Common Questions, Briefly

If the IRS audits an estate-tax return, what does that look like?

An IRS estate-tax audit typically begins with an examination letter requesting backup documentation for items reported on the Form 706 — appraisals, statements, valuation memoranda. The exam can take six months to two years. Most audits focus on valuation issues (closely held businesses, fractional interests, art, real property) rather than legal-inclusion questions. Settlement is the common path; only a small fraction of audits ripen into Tax Court litigation. Estates with material exposure should expect that significant valuation positions may face audit and should retain qualified appraisers whose work will withstand scrutiny.

Can the estate be insolvent — i.e., owe more tax than it has assets?

In rare cases yes, particularly when an estate consists primarily of illiquid assets (closely held businesses, real property) and lacks cash to pay the federal estate tax. Section 6166 provides for installment payment of estate tax attributable to a closely held business interest, spreading payments over up to fourteen years. Section 303 provides for redemption of corporate stock by the corporation to provide estate liquidity without the redemption being treated as a dividend. Specialist counsel can navigate these provisions for liquidity-constrained estates.

Chapter 2 takes up the estate-tax-versus-inheritance-tax distinction in detail. Chapter 3 explains why the system exists, in structural rather than political terms. Chapter 4 treats the gross estate — the question of what gets counted, which is where most of the actual surprise in tax practice lives. Together, these four chapters establish what estate tax is. The remainder of the book treats how it operates.

Figure 1.1

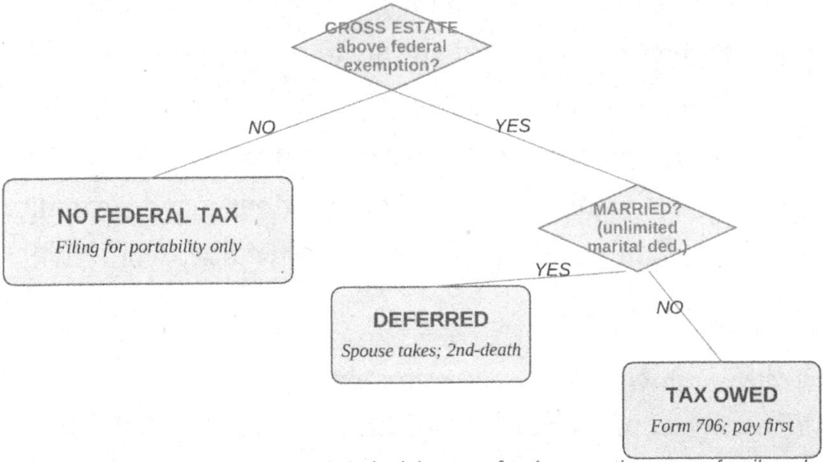

Will my estate owe federal estate tax? A decision tree for the question every family asks first.

KEY POINT

Estate tax is one part of a coordinated transfer-tax system. It is paid by the estate, not by beneficiaries. It is not income tax, not inheritance tax, and not automatic. Most American estates pay none. The system's first lesson is that fear is disproportionate to actual exposure for the great majority of families.

What This Chapter Has Said

Estate taxes are taxes on the transfer of wealth at death. They are imposed on the estate as a separate taxpayer, not on individual beneficiaries. They are categorically distinct from income tax, inheritance tax, capital-gains tax, gift tax, GST tax, and the various state-level taxes families confuse them with. Most American estates pay no federal estate tax under current law, and the entire system applies only when specific conditions are met. Understanding what the tax is and is not — categorically — is the foundation for everything that follows.

CHAPTER 2

Estate Tax vs. Inheritance Tax

Chapter at a Glance

- The structural distinction between estate tax (paid by estate) and inheritance tax (paid by beneficiary).
- Why the federal government has no inheritance tax — and which six states do.
- Why inheritance-tax rates depend on the relationship of the beneficiary to the deceased.
- Twelve states + DC with estate tax, and why state thresholds catch families well below federal exemption.
- Why a Florida estate and a Massachusetts estate of identical wealth produce different tax outcomes.

Estate taxes and inheritance taxes are often confused. They are not the same.

The confusion is partly linguistic — both phrases involve the word "tax," both involve a transfer of wealth at death, both are sometimes called "death taxes" in popular usage. The structural distinction is, however, crisp:

- Estate tax is assessed on the estate before distribution.

- Inheritance tax is assessed on beneficiaries after they receive property.

The federal government does not impose an inheritance tax. Six states do. Many states do not impose any death-related tax at all. Some states impose only an estate tax. Some impose only an inheritance tax. Two states impose both. Confusing these categories leads families to assume tax exposure where none exists — or, more dangerously, to miss exposure where it does.

Why the Distinction Matters Practically

Three practical consequences flow from the structural difference. Each is worth understanding before any planning decision is made.

(1) Who pays. Estate tax is paid by the estate — meaning, in practice, by the estate's executor, from estate assets, before any distribution to beneficiaries. Inheritance tax is paid by the beneficiary, from the property the beneficiary has received. The administrative burden falls on different people. The cash-flow consequences fall on different people. The exposure to audit and dispute falls on different people.

(2) Whether the relationship to the deceased matters. Estate taxes care about the estate's overall value and only secondarily about who receives it (with the marital deduction and charitable deduction as the principal exceptions). Inheritance taxes typically vary their rates by relationship — a spouse and

children may be exempt or taxed at low rates, while distant relatives and unrelated beneficiaries may face much higher rates on the same dollar. The same one-million-dollar bequest can produce zero inheritance tax in the hands of a child and substantial tax in the hands of a niece, in the same state under the same statute.

(3) Where the tax happens. Estate tax happens at the level of the estate's domiciliary state and the federal government. Inheritance tax happens at the level of the state where the deceased was domiciled (with various sourcing rules for out-of-state real property). The geography of exposure is different and produces different planning.

Table 2.1

Feature	Estate tax	Inheritance tax
Imposed on	The estate	The beneficiary
Paid by	Executor, from estate assets	Beneficiary, personally
Computed on	Gross estate (less deductions, exemption)	Property received by beneficiary
Rates depend on	Estate size	Relationship of beneficiary to deceased
Federal version exists	Yes (Form 706)	No
States with this tax (approx.)	12 states + DC	6 states
Marital deduction	Yes — unlimited	Typically yes — spouse exempt or low rate
Charitable deduction	Yes — unlimited	Typically yes — charitable beneficiary exempt
Spouse beneficiary	Generally non-taxable transfer	Generally exempt from inheritance tax
Distant relative beneficiary	Same — depends on estate size	Higher rates than for close relatives

Estate tax versus inheritance tax — a side-by-side comparison.

The Six Inheritance-Tax States

Six states currently impose an inheritance tax. The list is small enough to memorize, and it changes infrequently. As of writing, the inheritance-tax states are:

Table 2.2

State	Spouse rate	Children rate	Other beneficiaries
Iowa	Exempt	Exempt (statutory phase-out)	Tiered up to ~15% historically; phasing out
Kentucky	Exempt	Exempt	Class B (siblings) up to 16%; Class C (unrelated) up to 16%
Maryland	Exempt	Exempt	10% on most non-exempt beneficiaries
Nebraska	Exempt	1% (above small exemption)	Class 2 (relatives) 11%; Class 3 (unrelated) 15%
New Jersey	Exempt	Exempt	Class C (siblings) 11–16%; Class D (unrelated) 15–16%
Pennsylvania	Exempt	4.5%	Siblings 12%; other heirs 15%

Inheritance-tax states (representative; verify current law).

Two patterns in Table 2.2 are worth flagging. First, in every inheritance-tax state, the surviving spouse is fully exempt. This means the inheritance-tax exposure tends to fall on beneficiaries other than the spouse — typically children, grandchildren, siblings, or unrelated beneficiaries. Second, the rates rise sharply with the distance of the relationship. A bequest of a given amount to a niece in Pennsylvania may produce three to four times the tax of the same bequest to a child.

States With No Inheritance Tax (and No Estate Tax)

Approximately thirty-two states have neither an estate tax nor an inheritance tax. For families domiciled in these states, the transfer-tax exposure is essentially federal only — meaning that estates below the federal exemption face no transfer-tax liability at all. This is the simplest tax position, and it describes a substantial fraction of American families.

States with no transfer tax of either kind include (among others): Alabama, Alaska, Arizona, Arkansas, California, Colorado, Florida, Georgia, Idaho, Indiana, Kansas, Louisiana, Michigan, Mississippi, Missouri, Montana, Nevada, New Mexico, North Carolina, North Dakota, Ohio, Oklahoma, South Carolina, South Dakota, Tennessee, Texas, Utah, Virginia, West Virginia, Wisconsin, and Wyoming.

States With Estate Tax (but Not Inheritance Tax)

Approximately twelve states plus the District of Columbia impose an estate tax. We treat the state thresholds and rates in Chapter 5; for now, the relevant point is that the state estate-tax exemption is typically much lower than the federal exemption, sometimes by a factor of ten or twenty. A family comfortably below the federal threshold can be sharply exposed at the state level.

Table 2.3

State / DC	Approximate exemption	Notes
Connecticut	Federal level (matched)	Phased in to match federal.
District of Columbia	$4 million range	Indexed annually.
Hawaii	$5.5 million range	Pickup tax structure.
Illinois	$4 million	Cliff structure — exposure above threshold.
Maine	Federal level (matched)	Recently matched federal.
Maryland	$5 million	Imposes both estate tax AND inheritance tax.
Massachusetts	$2 million	Among the lowest thresholds.
Minnesota	$3 million range	Indexed.
New York	$6.94 million range	Cliff: above 105% of exemption, full estate taxed.
Oregon	$1 million	Lowest threshold among estate-tax states.
Rhode Island	$1.7 million range	Indexed.
Vermont	$5 million	Flat-rate above threshold.
Washington	$2.2 million range	Progressive rates.

States with estate tax — exemption thresholds (representative).

The Oregon and Massachusetts thresholds in particular catch families off guard. A two-million-dollar estate — by the standards of most American homeowners with retirement savings and a primary residence in an expensive metropolitan area, not an enormous estate — is fully exposed to state-level estate tax in those jurisdictions. Many residents have no awareness of this until they consult counsel.

> **REFLECTION**
>
> The geography of estate and inheritance taxes is uneven. A family of identical size and composition will face sharply different tax exposure depending on the state in which the deceased was domiciled at death. This is a structural feature of American federalism, not an oversight, and it rewards families that pay attention to domicile when their circumstances or family location is changing in late life.

What This Looks Like in Practice

Imagine two families of identical wealth — say, four million dollars — who die in the same week, one domiciled in Florida and one domiciled in Massachusetts. Both estates pass entirely to the deceased's children.

The Florida estate pays no federal estate tax (well below the federal exemption) and no state estate tax (Florida has none). Total transfer-tax liability: zero. The children receive four million dollars.

The Massachusetts estate also pays no federal estate tax. But Massachusetts maintains an estate tax with an exemption of roughly two million dollars. The Massachusetts estate-tax liability on a four-million-dollar estate is approximately $300,000 to $350,000 depending on the year and structure. The children receive somewhere between $3.65 and $3.7 million.

Same family size. Same wealth. Same direction of transfer. Roughly $300,000 difference, attributable entirely to the domicile state. This is what state-level exposure looks like in ordinary practice for families of moderate wealth.

What This Looks Like in Practice

Two estates — one in Pennsylvania, one in Delaware. Both decedents leave $500,000 each to a niece. Same amount. Same beneficiary type.

Pennsylvania imposes an inheritance tax. The deceased's niece, as a non-lineal beneficiary, faces a 15% inheritance-tax rate. Tax owed: $75,000. The niece receives a net $425,000.

Delaware has neither an estate tax nor an inheritance tax. The niece in Delaware receives the full $500,000.

Same family-relationship structure. Same dollar bequest. Same year. The state of domicile produced a $75,000 difference, paid by the niece personally. Neither estate filed a federal estate-tax return; both were below federal thresholds. The exposure was entirely state-level inheritance tax.

Where We Go From Here

Notes on Practice

The state-tax landscape changes more frequently than the federal. State legislatures revise thresholds, rates, and even the existence of estate or inheritance taxes regularly. A planning analysis done five years ago may already be obsolete in a state that has phased out its estate tax (Iowa) or one that has increased its threshold (Connecticut). Counsel should always verify current state law at the time of planning.

A second observation: domicile change for tax purposes is a real planning option for families with material state-level exposure approaching late life. The change must be genuine — driver's license, voter registration, primary residence, time spent — not merely a paper change. Half-hearted domicile changes fail audit consistently.

Practitioner Patterns — State-Specific Issues

Three state-specific patterns arise often enough to warrant explicit treatment.

First, the cliff-structure problem. Massachusetts and (in modified form) New York have used cliff structures under which crossing the threshold by even a dollar produces tax on the entire estate, not just the amount above. For estates near the threshold, this produces strong incentives to reduce the gross estate below the cliff — through marital and charitable transfers, basis-step-up planning, or other techniques. Massachusetts reformed its cliff in recent years to a more graduated structure; counsel should verify current state law before assuming the cliff applies.

Second, the state-level marital-deduction nuance. Most state estate-tax regimes follow the federal unlimited marital deduction, but some impose limits or additional requirements. For example, some states do not allow a state-level marital deduction for transfers to non-resident spouses or for QTIP-style marital trusts unless specific elections are made.

Counsel should not assume state rules track federal.

Third, the inheritance-tax-and-domicile interaction. Inheritance tax is imposed by the deceased's domiciliary state, not by the beneficiary's state of residence. A New Jersey beneficiary who inherits from a Pennsylvania decedent is subject to Pennsylvania inheritance tax, even though New Jersey has its own (now-repealed) inheritance tax. The deceased's domicile controls.

Domicile Change as a Planning Strategy

For families with material state-level exposure approaching late life, domicile change is sometimes a tractable planning option. The tax savings can be substantial — for high-net-worth families in high-tax states, moving to a no-estate-tax state can save millions of dollars in eventual transfer-tax liability.

But domicile change is not cosmetic. The classic indicia of domicile include physical presence, voter registration, driver's license, vehicle registration, primary residence, place of professional licensure, club memberships, religious and social affiliations, banking relationships, address used for tax filings, and the location where the family considers "home." States with material lost revenue from outmigration (notably New York and California) audit alleged domicile changes aggressively, and state revenue departments have increasingly sophisticated tools for asserting that a purported change was insufficient.

Successful domicile changes are usually multi-year processes: establishing presence in the new state, severing ties to the old state, documenting each step, and continuing the pattern without exceptions. Half-hearted changes (a new mailing address but continued residence in the prior state) routinely fail audit. Counsel handling domicile-change planning should engage the client's CPA, estate attorney, and the new state's counsel together to ensure the change is genuine and documented.

Common Questions, Briefly

If the deceased moved to Florida six months before death, did the move count?

Probably not, on its own. A six-month presence in Florida is consistent with seasonal residence rather than domicile change. The high-tax originating state will likely assert continued domicile, and the burden will be on the estate to prove otherwise. Whether the move counts depends on the totality of evidence — including pre-move planning, severance of ties to the prior state, and contemporaneous documentation. Late-life moves for tax purposes alone, made hastily, frequently fail audit.

Does a state estate tax apply to property the deceased owned in another state?

Generally yes for the deceased's domicile state, with credit or apportionment relief for tax paid on the same property to another state. Real property in particular is subject to ancillary state-level estate tax in the situs state under many state regimes. The interaction between domiciliary tax and ancillary tax is technical; specialist counsel familiar with both states' law is necessary for any estate with multi-state real property.

Chapter 3 takes up the policy structure: why these taxes exist, what they are designed to do, and why understanding their structural rationale helps clarify when they will and will not apply to a particular family. Chapter 4 then turns to the gross estate — the question that, more than any other, determines whether and how much tax is owed.

Figure 2.1

WHAT ESTATE TAX IS *Federal & state-level*	WHAT ESTATE TAX IS NOT *Common confusions*
• Tax on transfer of wealth at death	• Income tax (separate Form 1041)
• Imposed on the estate	• Inheritance tax (paid by beneficiary)
• Paid before distribution	• Capital-gains tax (sale event)
• Filed on Form 706	• Automatic tax on every estate
• Below-threshold estates pay none	• A 50% confiscation
• 12 states + DC have state version	• Required for most US deaths

Estate tax versus inheritance tax — what each is, who pays, and where each applies.

KEY POINT

Estate tax is paid by the estate; inheritance tax is paid by the beneficiary. The federal government has no inheritance tax. Twelve states + DC have estate tax; six states have inheritance tax. Two regimes are structurally different and require different planning. State-level exposure is broader than federal.

What This Chapter Has Said

The estate-tax versus inheritance-tax distinction is structural, not cosmetic. Estate tax falls on the estate; inheritance tax falls on the beneficiary. Federal law has no inheritance tax. State law varies. Twelve states + DC maintain estate taxes. Six states maintain inheritance taxes. Maryland imposes both. The geography of exposure shapes planning more than most families realize.

PART II

◆

STRUCTURAL DESIGN

Why the system exists and what it actually counts.

CHAPTER 3

Why Estate Taxes Exist

Chapter at a Glance

- The three structural concerns the transfer-tax system addresses: concentration, coordination, time-shifting.
- Why estate tax is principally a regulatory tax, not a fiscal one — federal receipts are a fraction of one percent.
- Why the rules that look strange (marital deduction, GST, inclusion under §2036) are responses to specific structural problems.
- Why the system is designed to be planned around within limits.
- Why most American estates pay no federal estate tax — and what fraction actually do.

Estate taxes exist for structural reasons, not moral ones.

Reasonable people disagree about whether the system, in its current form, achieves its goals or whether it should exist at all. Those debates are political and well-documented. This chapter does not attempt to resolve them. Its purpose is more modest: to explain what the transfer-tax system was designed to do, structurally, so that readers can understand its particular features as the responses to particular structural problems rather than as arbitrary impositions.

Estate and gift taxes, as a system, are designed to:

- regulate the transfer of large accumulations of wealth between generations
- prevent indefinite concentration of property within a single family across multiple generations
- operate as part of a coordinated transfer-tax system that prevents avoidance through timing alone
- raise revenue, though this has become a minor function of the federal system over the past forty years

Estate taxes are not a judgment on families. They are a policy tool that applies only when thresholds and conditions are met. Most estates do not pay federal estate tax.

The Three Structural Concerns the System Addresses

The current American transfer-tax system is built around three structural concerns that are worth naming directly.

(1) Concentration across generations. American policy has, at various points and through various instruments, expressed a preference against the indefinite concentration of wealth within a single family line. The estate tax is one instrument of that preference. The generation-skipping transfer tax is another. Whether either tax achieves the policy goal effectively is contested; that the goal exists, in the structure, is not.

Understanding this rationale explains features that would otherwise seem strange — the unlimited marital deduction (transfers within a generation are not the concern), the generation-skipping rules (skipping the children to give to grandchildren is treated as a separate tax event), the preferential treatment of charitable transfers (which remove wealth from concentration entirely).

(2) Coordination across the lifetime/at-death boundary. If transfer tax applied only at death, every family with material exposure would simply give wealth away during life and avoid the tax entirely. The system anticipates this by imposing a parallel gift tax that uses the same exemption pool. Lifetime gifts use up the same applicable exclusion amount that would otherwise shelter the estate at death. This coordination — the unified credit — is the reason the gift-tax and estate-tax systems must be understood together. We treat the unified credit in Chapter 7.

(3) Time-shifting through control. If a family could transfer assets while retaining all the practical benefits — income, occupancy, control over disposition — the transfer would be a transfer in name only. The system anticipates this with a series of inclusion rules under Internal Revenue Code sections 2036 through 2042 that pull back into the gross estate any property over which the deceased retained particular powers. These rules are the source of most of the surprise inclusions in actual

estate-tax practice. We treat them in Chapter 4.

Revenue Is Not the Principal Purpose

It is worth noting, against a common assumption, that the federal estate tax is not principally a revenue measure in the current American fiscal system. Federal estate-tax receipts have hovered, for decades, between a few billion and a few tens of billions of dollars annually — meaningful in absolute terms but a fraction of one percent of total federal revenue. The system is in this sense a regulatory tax rather than a fiscal one: its principal effect is on the structure of wealth transfer rather than on the federal balance sheet.

Different American states have taken different positions on the same question. Some maintain robust estate or inheritance taxes that produce material state revenue. Others have repealed their estate taxes entirely on the grounds that the regulatory function is adequately served at the federal level and that maintaining a state-level overlay drives wealthy residents to relocate. This is a live policy debate in many states and produces periodic threshold and rate adjustments.

What This Means for Planning

Two practical consequences follow from understanding the system's structural rationale.

First, the rules that look strange usually are not. The unlimited marital deduction, the generation-skipping rules, the inclusion provisions for retained interests, the valuation discounts and disallowances, the unified credit between gift and estate tax — each of these is the response to a specific structural problem the system is trying to solve. Treating them as arbitrary leads to bad planning. Treating them as structural responses leads to better planning.

Second, the system is designed to be planned around — within limits. The exemptions are set at levels that exempt most estates entirely. The unlimited marital deduction allows spouses to defer all federal estate tax on the first death. The annual gift-tax exclusion permits substantial lifetime transfers without using lifetime exemption. The basis-step-up rule (treated in Chapters 8 and 9) is the most generous income-tax provision in the entire Code for inherited property. Families that engage with the structure tend to achieve favorable outcomes; families that resist or ignore the structure tend to be surprised.

KEY POINT

The transfer-tax system is a coordinated regulatory framework, not a single tax. Understanding its structural rationale — concentration, coordination, time-shifting — explains its features and supports better planning. Most of what looks arbitrary in the system is actually a structural response to a specific concern.

Most Estates Do Not Pay Federal Estate Tax

It is worth ending this chapter with a fact that frequently surprises readers and that anchors much of the remaining discussion: the federal estate tax, in its current form, applies to a small minority of American deaths. Estimates from the IRS Statistics of Income division, the Tax Policy Center, and academic researchers consistently put the share of deaths producing a federal estate-tax filing obligation at roughly 0.1 to 0.2 percent of all American decedents. The share producing actual federal estate tax owed is even lower.

What This Looks Like in Practice

A husband and wife with substantial wealth — call them Edward and Margaret — visit an estate-planning attorney for the first time at age sixty. They have heard that estate taxes are something they need to worry about. They are open to planning.

The attorney walks them through the structural logic of the transfer-tax system rather than through specific planning structures first. Edward and Margaret learn that the system is designed to permit unlimited transfers between them, to permit substantial annual gifts to children, to permit transfers to charity, and to apply tax only to net wealth above the federal exemption. They learn that the inclusion rules are designed to prevent transfers that are transfers in name only.

Armed with this structural understanding, Edward and Margaret make different decisions than they would have. They start annual-exclusion gifting to their three children and seven grandchildren. They structure their wills with credit-shelter trusts to preserve both exemptions at the state level. They purchase life insurance through an ILIT rather than individually. None of these moves is exotic. All of them are responses to the structural framework. Over twenty years, they reduce their projected federal estate-tax exposure by approximately seven million dollars.

Couples who engage with the structural logic early almost always do better than couples who try to plan reactively at the end. The lesson is not complicated. The discipline of starting early is.

Most American families will not face federal estate tax under the current threshold. State-level exposure is broader but still affects a minority of families. The fear is disproportionate to the actual frequency. The fear is primarily about not knowing which side of the threshold a particular family is on, and what gets counted in computing the comparison.

Notes on Practice

The structural rationale for the transfer-tax system is worth explaining to clients early because it produces better planning conversations. Clients who see the system as a coordinated framework with specific concerns engage with it productively. Clients who see the system as arbitrary often resist planning that would actually serve them well.

A second observation: the political volatility of the federal estate tax — periodic exemption increases, scheduled sunsets, threats of repeal or expansion — is real and affects long-term planning. Planners should build flexibility into structures so that they remain useful under different exemption levels. Locking in a structure that only works at one exemption level is a planning failure.

Practitioner Patterns — The Politics of Tax Volatility

Three observations about the political volatility of the federal estate tax shape long-term planning.

First, the federal exemption has changed dramatically over the past four decades. From a low of $600k in the 1980s, through several increases in the 1990s and 2000s, to the current high level. Scheduled changes (sunset provisions) make the exemption a moving target. Planning structures should be designed to function under multiple exemption scenarios rather than locked to one specific level. The credit-shelter (bypass) trust is the classic flexible structure: it absorbs whatever exemption is available at the first death, regardless of the specific level. Trusts drafted with hard-coded dollar amounts (e.g., "the first $5 million to the bypass trust") fail when the exemption moves; trusts drafted with formula clauses (e.g., "the deceased's available exemption equivalent") adapt automatically.

Second, the political coalitions affecting the transfer-tax system are unusual. Estate tax is supported across portions of the political spectrum for very different reasons (revenue, regulatory concentration, social-equity arguments) and opposed from similarly varied positions. The result is policy that moves in fits and starts. Long-term planning must accommodate uncertainty. Most experienced planners build structures that work under both higher and lower exemption scenarios, rather than betting on one outcome.

Third, state-level policy moves on its own clock. States have variously raised, lowered, or repealed their estate and inheritance taxes over the past two decades. The state landscape is more dynamic than the federal. Annual review of state-level exposure should be part of any serious planning engagement for clients with state-level concerns. Connecticut and Maine have moved to federal-equivalent thresholds in recent years; Iowa is phasing out its inheritance tax; Hawaii adopted estate tax in the past two decades. The landscape will continue to shift.

Why the System Looks Strange

Three structural features of the system look strange to non-specialists and have specific structural rationales worth understanding:

(1) Why is there an unlimited marital deduction but no unlimited child or sibling deduction? The marital deduction exists because the system treats married couples as a single

economic unit; transfers within the unit are not the kind of concentration the system is concerned with. Transfers across the unit (to children, siblings, etc.) are the kind of intergenerational concentration the system is designed to address. The marital deduction is a generational-coordination mechanism, not a relationship-based generosity.

(2) Why is there a generation-skipping transfer tax in addition to the estate tax? Without it, families could transfer wealth from grandparent to grandchild, avoiding the estate-tax event at the parent's death entirely. The GST tax ensures that wealth is taxed at each generational transfer, not just selectively. The GST exemption (set at the same level as the estate-tax exemption) provides parallel exemption relief.

(3) Why are charitable transfers unlimitedly deductible? Charitable transfers remove wealth from family lines entirely; they do not produce intergenerational concentration. The system is structurally indifferent to the charitable use and rewards it with full deduction. The various charitable vehicles (CRTs, CLTs, private foundations) provide different ways to combine charitable transfers with limited family benefits.

Common Questions, Briefly

Why does the federal estate tax raise so little revenue if the rate is 40%?

Three reasons. First, the high exemption ($13+ million per individual at the time of writing) means most estates pay no tax. Second, the unlimited marital deduction defers all first-death tax for married couples. Third, sophisticated planning structures (annual gifts, GRATs, valuation discounts, charitable transfers) reduce the taxable estates of the wealthy. The combination is that even with a 40% top rate, the federal estate tax raises only a fraction of one percent of total federal revenue. The system is principally regulatory, not fiscal.

Those that do face the tax tend to be surprised not by the tax itself, but by what was included. That is the subject of Chapter 4.

Figure 3.1

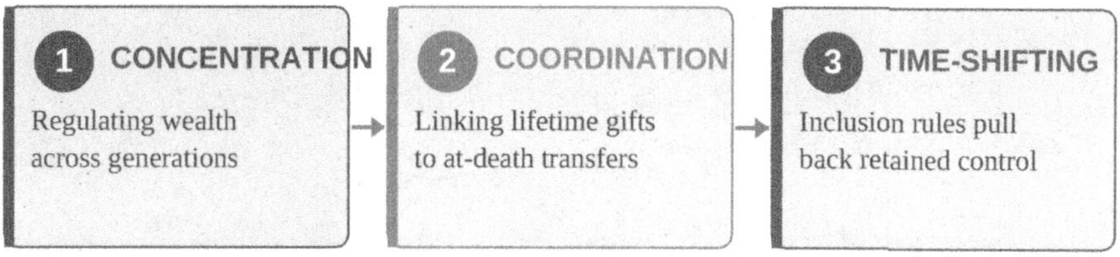

The three structural concerns of the transfer-tax system — concentration, coordination, time-shifting.

> **KEY POINT**
>
> The transfer-tax system is a coordinated regulatory framework with specific structural goals. Most of its features are responses to identifiable structural concerns. Treating the system as arbitrary leads to bad planning. Treating it as a structural framework supports better outcomes.

What This Chapter Has Said

The transfer-tax system addresses three structural concerns: concentration of wealth across generations, coordination across the lifetime/at-death boundary, and time-shifting through retained control. Federal estate tax is principally a regulatory tax. Most American estates pay none. The system is designed to be planned around within limits. Engagement with the structure produces favorable outcomes; resistance to it produces surprises.

CHAPTER 4

What Gets Counted in an Estate

Chapter at a Glance

- Why the gross estate is broader than the probate estate — sometimes much broader.
- Life insurance under §2042 — the most common surprise inclusion, with the ILIT cure.
- Retained interests under §2036 — the parent-keeps-living-in-the-house pattern.
- Powers of appointment under §2041 — general versus limited, and why the distinction matters.
- Joint property — full inclusion for non-spouse joints unless contribution is proved; 50/50 for spouses.
- Pre-death gifts and the three-year lookback under §2035.

Estate taxes are based on the gross estate, not the probate estate.

This is where the actual confusion in estate-tax practice begins. Most families, when asked to estimate the value of an estate, instinctively count the assets that would pass through probate — house, bank accounts, brokerage accounts, individually owned property. That is the probate estate. The gross estate — the basis on which federal estate tax is computed

— is broader, sometimes much broader.

The gross estate includes:

- assets owned outright at the moment of death
- assets held in revocable trusts the deceased could amend or revoke
- assets over which the deceased retained substantial control or beneficial enjoyment
- certain transferred assets pulled back into the estate by statutory inclusion rules
- life-insurance proceeds the deceased owned the policy on (or had specific incidents of ownership over)
- the deceased's interest in jointly held property (in proportions determined by the form of joint ownership)
- the value of certain annuities and pension benefits payable at or after death

What matters is not where assets sit, but whether control existed at death. This explains why estates can be larger for tax purposes than families expect.

The Difference Between Gross Estate and Probate Estate

Before we treat the inclusion rules in detail, the structural distinction between gross estate and probate estate deserves an explicit table.

Table 4.1

Asset type	Probate estate	Gross estate
House in deceased's individual name	Yes	Yes
House in joint tenancy with spouse	No (transfers automatically)	Half (or per contribution rule)
House in revocable living trust	No (transfers per trust)	Yes — full inclusion
Brokerage account, single name	Yes	Yes
IRA / 401(k) with named beneficiary	No (passes by beneficiary designation)	Yes — full inclusion
Life insurance, deceased owned policy	No (passes by beneficiary designation)	Yes — full death benefit
Life insurance, irrevocable trust owns policy	No	No (if deceased had no incidents of ownership)
Joint bank account, with adult child	No (passes to surviving co-owner)	Full value, unless child contributed
Lifetime gift made within 3 years of death	No	Yes (gift tax "gross-up" rule, IRC §2035)
Property given away with retained life estate	No	Yes — full date-of-death value (§2036)
Power-of-appointment trust	No (deceased was not legal owner)	Yes if deceased held a general power of appointment (§2041)

Probate estate vs. gross estate — what each counts.

Several of the rows in Table 4.1 deserve closer examination because they are the source of most surprise inclusions in ordinary practice.

Life Insurance — The Most Common Surprise

Of all the inclusion rules, the treatment of life insurance produces the most consistent surprise. Most families assume that because life insurance proceeds pass directly to a named beneficiary outside probate, those proceeds are also outside the estate for tax purposes. They are not.

Under Internal Revenue Code section 2042, life-insurance proceeds payable on the deceased's life are includible in the gross estate if the deceased held any "incidents of ownership" over the policy at death. "Incidents of ownership" is a term of art that includes virtually any control over the policy — the right to change the beneficiary, the right to surrender the policy for cash value, the right to assign or pledge the policy, the right to borrow against the policy, even certain reversionary interests.

If the deceased was the named insured AND owned the policy (in any of the senses above), the full death benefit is includible in the gross estate at the deceased's date of death — not the cash surrender value, but the death benefit actually paid. For families with substantial life insurance, this can dramatically increase the gross estate.

The cure is straightforward but must be implemented during life: hold the policy in an irrevocable life-insurance trust (commonly abbreviated ILIT) so that the deceased never personally holds incidents of ownership. The trust holds the policy. The trust pays the premiums (using funds typically gifted to the trust subject to annual exclusion). The trust is named as beneficiary. On the insured's death, the proceeds are paid to the trust and are not includible in the insured's estate.

Implemented during life, this structure can keep multi-million-dollar life insurance policies entirely outside the taxable estate. Implemented too late — within three years of death — the inclusion rule of section 2035 pulls the proceeds back in regardless of the trust structure. Timing matters.

Retained Interests — The Section 2036 Rule

Internal Revenue Code section 2036 is the second-most-common source of surprise inclusions. The rule applies when the deceased made a transfer of property during life but retained a substantial interest in or power over the transferred property. The classic example: a parent transfers the family home to children but continues to live in it without paying fair-market rent. Section 2036 includes the home in the parent's gross estate at full date-of-death value, regardless of the gift made years earlier.

The rule is structural rather than punitive. It exists to prevent transfers that are transfers in name only — where the deceased gave property away but kept all the practical benefits. The cure is to make the transfer real: the parent either pays fair-market rent to the children or vacates the property. Either approach disposes of the section 2036 issue. Continuing to occupy without rent does not.

Powers of Appointment — The Section 2041 Rule

A power of appointment is the right to direct property held in trust to particular beneficiaries. The deceased may have such a power even when the deceased is not the trust's beneficial owner. Internal Revenue Code section 2041 includes in the deceased's gross estate any property over which the deceased held a "general" power of appointment at death — meaning a power exercisable in favor of the deceased, the deceased's estate, the deceased's creditors, or creditors of the deceased's estate.

Powers of appointment that are limited (e.g., exercisable only in favor of the deceased's descendants other than the deceased) are not general powers and do not produce inclusion. The distinction is technical but important; irrevocable trusts intended to keep property outside the successor's estate must be drafted with limited powers, not general powers.

Joint Property — Inclusion by Contribution and by Form

Joint property is included in the gross estate under one of two rules, depending on the form.

For property held jointly with a non-spouse — adult children, siblings, business partners — the full value is included in the deceased's estate except to the extent the survivor can prove independent contribution. This is the "contribution rule" of Internal Revenue Code section 2040(a). It produces surprising results: a parent who titles the family home jointly with an adult child for probate-avoidance purposes produces a full inclusion in the parent's estate, because the child made no contribution to the original purchase. The joint titling did not reduce the gross estate; it merely avoided probate.

For property held jointly with a spouse, a different rule applies. Under section 2040(b), spousal joint property is treated as 50% includible in each spouse's estate, regardless of contribution. This is the "qualified joint interest" rule. It simplifies administration and matches the income-tax treatment in non-community-property states.

Pre-Death Gifts — The Three-Year Rule

Internal Revenue Code section 2035 includes in the gross estate certain transfers made within three years of death. The rule does not apply to all gifts (most lifetime gifts remain outside the gross estate even if made shortly before death) but does apply specifically to:

- Transfers of life insurance policies on the deceased's life (which is why ILIT formation must occur more than three years before death to be fully effective);
- Gift tax paid on transfers made within three years of death (the "gross-up" rule that prevents discounted-tax planning);
- Transfers that would have been includible under sections 2036, 2037, 2038, or 2042 if not for the inter-vivos transfer.

Most other lifetime gifts are completely outside the gross estate even when made days before death. The three-year rule is narrow but catches the planning steps that would otherwise be most valuable.

> **REFLECTION**
>
> The gross estate is what control looks like at death, translated into a tax base. Property the deceased actually owned, property the deceased could have owned by asserting a power, property the deceased gave away while keeping the benefits — all of these reflect a kind of ongoing control that the tax system treats as the same category. Understanding this principle is more useful than memorizing the section numbers.

What This Looks Like in Practice

Consider a hypothetical estate. The deceased — call her Margaret — was a widow at age eighty-one with what she thought of as modest holdings. Her probate estate (assets in her individual name) was about $1.8 million: her home in Massachusetts ($900,000), her brokerage account ($600,000), her bank accounts ($150,000), and personal property ($150,000).

Margaret's children, anticipating the estate administration, were not concerned about federal estate tax. The probate estate was well below the federal exemption.

When the gross estate was computed, the picture changed. Margaret's IRA, with her three children as named beneficiaries, held $1.4 million. Margaret had been the owner of a $1 million life-insurance policy on her own life, with her children as beneficiaries — the policy paid out outside probate. Margaret had transferred her vacation home to a family LLC eight years earlier but continued to use it without paying rent — the IRS asserted section 2036 inclusion at $750,000. Margaret had been a co-trustee of a trust her late husband had funded, with a power to direct principal to herself for support — the IRS asserted section 2041 inclusion at $1.2 million.

Margaret's gross estate, as ultimately computed, was approximately $6.2 million, not the $1.8 million the family had expected. This was below the federal exemption and produced no federal estate tax. But it was sharply above the Massachusetts state estate-tax threshold, producing approximately $500,000 of state estate-tax liability.

Each of the inclusions was foreseeable. Each had a planning cure available during life. None of the cures was implemented. The Massachusetts tax was the result.

Margaret's family is a composite, but the pattern is extremely common. Most surprise estate-tax exposure traces to what got counted, not to what people knew about the exemption.

What This Looks Like in Practice

A widow — call her Margaret — was an eighty-one-year-old homeowner in Massachusetts. Her children, knowing the federal exemption was high, did not expect estate-tax exposure. They thought of her estate as her home, her brokerage account, and her bank balance — together about $1.8 million. Below the federal exemption. Below, they assumed, any state threshold of concern.

When the gross estate was actually computed, the picture changed. Margaret's IRA, with her three children as beneficiaries, held $1.4 million. Margaret had owned a $1 million life-insurance policy on her own life — the policy paid out outside probate but was fully includible for tax purposes under §2042. Margaret had transferred her vacation home to a family LLC eight years earlier but continued to use it without paying rent — the IRS asserted §2036 inclusion at $750,000. Margaret had been a co-trustee of a trust her late husband had funded, with a power to direct principal to herself for support — the IRS asserted §2041 inclusion at $1.2 million.

Margaret's gross estate, as ultimately computed, was approximately $6.2 million. Below federal exemption — no federal tax. But sharply above the Massachusetts state estate-tax threshold, producing approximately $500,000 of state estate-tax liability.

Each of the inclusions was foreseeable. Each had a planning cure available during life. None had been implemented. The Massachusetts tax was the result. Margaret's family is a composite, but the pattern is extremely common. Most surprise estate-tax exposure traces to what got counted, not to what people knew about the exemption.

Where We Go From Here

Notes on Practice

The single most useful intake question in estate-tax planning is: "Tell me about your life insurance." Families consistently underweight the inclusion of life insurance in the gross estate. The cure (an ILIT) must be implemented more than three years before death. Counsel should ask the question early in any engagement so that the structure can be implemented with adequate runway.

A second observation: section 2036 inclusion based on retained interests is highly fact-specific. The IRS asserts inclusion in cases where the retained interest is informal — the parent who continues to live in the gifted home, the donor who continues to use the gifted vacation property. Documenting the absence of retention (rent paid, exclusive use by donee) is essential. Sloppy documentation creates audit risk.

Practitioner Patterns — Inclusion Subtleties

Three inclusion patterns deserve closer treatment because they recur in actual audit practice.

First, the indirect-benefits problem under §2036. The IRS has asserted §2036 inclusion in cases where the deceased had no formal retained interest but continued to receive practical benefits — the founder who continued drawing a salary from a transferred family business, the donor who continued to occupy a transferred residence even paying below-market rent, the settlor whose lifestyle was supported by trust distributions even where the trust agreement did not formally guarantee them. These cases turn on facts and circumstances. Documentation of arms-length pricing and clear separation of practical use is essential to defend non-inclusion.

Second, the powers-of-appointment subtleties under §2041. A general power of appointment includes any power exercisable in favor of the holder, the holder's estate, the holder's creditors, or creditors of the holder's estate. Trust drafting must avoid all four formulations to keep a power limited. The HEMS standard ("health, education, maintenance, and support") used in many trusts is an ascertainable standard that does NOT make a power general — but only if the standard is actually drafted as a HEMS standard, not as a broader discretionary power. Drafting precision matters.

Third, the IRA inclusion question. IRAs are fully includible in the gross estate of the participant. Beneficiary designations control distribution, not inclusion. Families that assume an IRA is "outside" the estate because it has a named beneficiary are wrong on the inclusion question — though right on the probate-administration question. Distinguish the two.

The Closely Held Business Inclusion Problem

For families whose wealth is concentrated in a closely held business — operating company, real estate holdings, family partnership — inclusion in the gross estate produces several specific issues that warrant explicit treatment.

First, valuation. Closely held businesses do not have public market prices. Valuation requires a qualified appraisal applying recognized methodologies (income approach, market approach, asset approach) with supporting documentation. The IRS aggressively scrutinizes valuation reports, particularly those claiming significant minority-interest or lack-of-marketability discounts. Counsel should engage appraisers with documented IRS-defense experience.

Second, valuation discounts. Minority-interest discounts and lack-of-marketability discounts have historically reduced reported values by 20–45% for closely held interests. The IRS has challenged aggressive discounts repeatedly; the Tax Court has been inconsistent. Recent guidance (the 2016 proposed and later withdrawn §2704 regulations, the subsequent legislative attention) has produced uncertainty. Discounts remain available but should be supported by qualified appraisal and grounded in market evidence.

Third, liquidity. The estate may owe substantial estate tax but lack cash to pay it. Section 6166 permits installment payment over up to fourteen years for estate tax attributable to a qualifying closely held business interest. Section 303 permits the corporation to redeem stock from the estate without dividend treatment. These provisions, properly invoked, can solve the liquidity problem; missed, they can force the family into distressed sales.

Common Questions, Briefly

If I sold a property to a family member at fair market value during life, is it in my gross estate?

Generally no, if the sale was genuine — fair-market price, documented, with consideration actually paid. The §2036 inclusion rule applies to gifts and below-market transfers where the donor retained a substantial interest. A fair-market sale is not a gift and does not produce §2036 inclusion. The proceeds of the sale, of course, become part of the seller's other assets and are included if still on hand at death.

What if I lent money to my children — is the loan in my gross estate?

Yes, the outstanding loan balance is in the lender's gross estate as a receivable. If the loan is forgiven during the lender's life, the forgiveness is a gift subject to gift tax. If the loan is forgiven at death (through a will provision), the loan balance is includible in the gross estate but the forgiveness operates as a bequest. Intra-family loans should carry market-rate interest (the AFR — applicable federal rate) and be documented as genuine loans; otherwise the IRS may recharacterize the original transfer as a gift.

Chapter 5 takes up the exemption system itself — federal and state — and explains why the inclusion question almost always matters more than the exemption number. With the gross estate established, the exemption is mechanical; the interesting and consequential decisions are upstream of it.

Figure 4.1

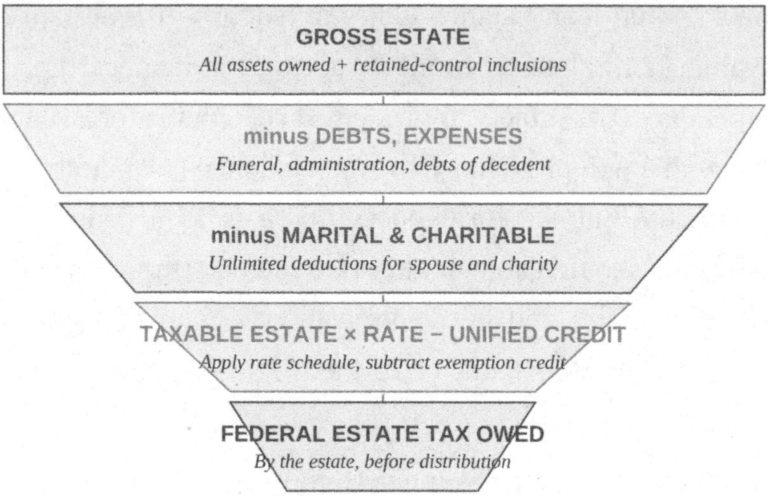

How the gross estate becomes federal estate tax — the computational funnel from inclusion to tax owed.

KEY POINT

Most surprise estate-tax exposure traces to what got counted in the gross estate, not to what the family knew about the exemption. Sections 2035 through 2042 produce most of the surprise inclusions. Each has a specific cure available during life.

What This Chapter Has Said

The gross estate is broader than the probate estate. Inclusion rules under sections 2035 through 2042 reach property the deceased did not technically own at death. The cures are specific and structural — ILITs, true transfers with rent or vacation, limited rather than general powers, careful titling, and early implementation. Each surprise is preventable; the prevention requires engagement during life.

PART III

THE EXEMPTION SYSTEM

Why the exemption number matters less than the inclusion question — and what each level of government allows.

CHAPTER 5

The Estate Tax Exemption

Chapter at a Glance

- How the federal exemption actually works — applied as a credit after the rate computation.
- Why the inclusion question matters more than the exemption number.
- Portability (DSUE) — what it does, why it must be timely elected, and what it does not cover.
- Why state-level exemption thresholds are typically much lower than federal — Oregon at $1m, Massachusetts at $2m.
- Cliff structures versus smooth thresholds, and how they shape planning near the threshold.

The estate tax exemption — formally the applicable exclusion amount under Internal Revenue Code section 2010 — is the dollar amount of taxable estate that can pass to non-spouse, non-charitable beneficiaries without producing federal estate tax.

This number changes over time. It has been as low as $675,000 in recent decades and is, at the time of writing, in the low- to mid-eight figures per individual (with a doubled amount available to married couples through portability). The current high level is the result of legislative changes that are scheduled to sunset; absent further legislation, the exemption will return to a substantially lower level. Specific current figures are not stated in this volume because they will change.

Many people believe being "below the exemption" means estate taxes do not matter. That belief is incomplete.

The exemption applies after inclusion is determined. If assets are included in the gross estate (per the rules of Chapter 4), they are counted first. The exemption is applied later. Understanding inclusion matters more than memorizing the exemption amount.

How the Exemption Actually Works

The federal exemption is structured as a credit against tax, not as a deduction from the taxable base. The mechanics matter because they explain why a small change in inclusion can produce a sharp change in tax owed near the threshold.

The computation, simplified, runs:

1. **Determine the gross estate.** Per the inclusion rules treated in Chapter 4.
2. **Apply allowable deductions.** Marital deduction, charitable deduction, debts and expenses, state death taxes paid (limited).
3. **Add adjusted taxable gifts.** Lifetime gifts that used the unified credit pool — these are added back to compute the

tax.

4. **Compute the tentative tax.** Apply the federal estate-tax rate schedule (which begins at 18% and rises to 40% on the highest portions) to the sum of the taxable estate plus adjusted taxable gifts.

5. **Subtract the unified credit.** The credit equivalent of the applicable exclusion amount. If the gross estate (plus adjusted gifts) is below the exemption equivalent, the credit covers the entire tentative tax and no estate tax is owed.

6. **Subtract other credits.** Foreign death taxes, prior-transfer credit, and similar narrower provisions.

What this structure means in practice: the exemption is not subtracted from the gross estate before the rates are applied. Instead, the rates are applied to the entire taxable estate plus adjusted gifts, and the unified credit shelters the first portion. The result is the same, but the mechanics matter for understanding portability (treated below) and for understanding why valuation discounts and inclusion arguments are so consequential.

Portability — The Unused Spouse's Exemption

Internal Revenue Code section 2010(c)(4) provides that a surviving spouse may claim the unused portion of the deceased spouse's federal exemption — formally, the deceased spousal unused exclusion amount, abbreviated DSUE. This is the rule known as "portability," and it is one of the most consequential planning features of the modern federal system.

The mechanics, simplified: when one spouse dies, the executor can elect, on a timely-filed Form 706, to make the deceased spouse's unused exemption available to the surviving spouse. The surviving spouse can then use both the deceased spouse's DSUE and their own exemption against their own eventual estate. The combined effect is to roughly double the available exemption for the married couple's combined lifetime and at-death transfers.

Three points about portability deserve explicit treatment because each catches families off guard.

First, portability requires a timely filing. The Form 706 must be filed within nine months of death (extendible to fifteen months) even if no estate tax is owed. A surviving spouse cannot claim portability years later; the election is made on the first-spouse-to-die's return or it is lost. The IRS has, in recent years, granted extended relief in some cases, but the safest path is timely filing.

Second, portability does not apply to the generation-skipping transfer tax. The GST exemption is not portable. Married couples that wish to use both spouses' GST exemptions must do so through trust structures (typically a credit-shelter or bypass trust) rather than relying on portability.

Third, portability does not apply to most state estate taxes. State portability is uneven; some states (Hawaii, Maryland) recognize a state-level DSUE, others do not. Families with state-level exposure should plan around the state's own rules rather than assuming federal portability extends down.

The State Exemption Landscape

We treated the state-by-state estate-tax exemption thresholds in Table 2.3 (Chapter 2). Three additional patterns are worth naming here because they shape planning meaningfully.

(1) State exemptions are typically much lower than the federal. Where the federal exemption is in the high seven or eight figures, state exemptions of $1 million (Oregon), $2 million (Massachusetts, Washington), and $4-5 million (Illinois, Maryland, Vermont, DC) catch families that have no federal exposure at all. The same family can be comfortably below the federal threshold and sharply exposed at the state level.

(2) Some states use a cliff structure rather than a smooth above-threshold structure. A cliff means that when the estate exceeds the threshold even by a dollar, the entire estate (not just

the portion above) becomes subject to tax. Massachusetts historically used a cliff structure (recently reformed); Oregon has used a partial cliff; New York uses a modified cliff (full estate taxed when value exceeds 105% of exemption). Cliff structures dramatically change the marginal cost of additional inclusion and produce strong planning incentives near the threshold.

(3) Some states do not recognize federal portability. A married couple in a state without state-level portability must use both exemptions through trust structures or risk wasting the first-spouse-to-die's state exemption. This is the dominant reason credit-shelter trusts (also called "bypass" or "family" trusts) remain in widespread use despite federal portability.

Why Inclusion Matters More Than the Exemption Amount

We have argued throughout this chapter that the exemption is mechanically applied after inclusion is determined. This structural fact has a practical consequence worth stating directly: in actual estate-tax practice, virtually all of the interesting decisions are about what gets included, not about the exemption number.

If your gross estate is well below the exemption, no amount of optimization changes the result; you owe no tax. If your gross estate is well above the exemption, no amount of exemption-focused thinking helps; the question is whether valid inclusion arguments or planning structures can reduce the gross estate. The interesting territory is the middle: estates near the threshold where small inclusion changes can make the difference between tax and no tax.

This is why the inclusion rules of Chapter 4, the gift-tax interaction of Chapter 7, and the basis-step-up rules of Chapters 8 and 9 are far more consequential to ordinary estate-tax practice than the exemption number itself. A family that focuses entirely on the exemption — "are we above or below?" — is asking the wrong question.

> **KEY POINT**
>
> The federal exemption is mechanically applied after inclusion is determined. Most of the planning value in estate-tax work is upstream of the exemption — in what gets counted, in how lifetime gifts interact with the at-death calculation, and in how basis is preserved. Treating the exemption as the central question misses where the real decisions are.

What This Looks Like in Practice

Two married couples, both with combined estates of approximately $4 million. Couple A is domiciled in Florida; Couple B is domiciled in Massachusetts. Both couples die in the same year (the husbands first, the wives second, four years later).

Couple A — Florida. The husband's death produces no estate tax (well below federal exemption, no Florida estate tax). The executor still files Form 706 to elect portability, preserving the husband's unused federal exemption for the wife. The wife dies four years later with the combined estate (now $4.3 million after growth). Her estate is well below the doubled federal exemption. No federal tax. No Florida tax. The children inherit $4.3 million.

Couple B — Massachusetts. The husband's death produces no federal estate tax (well below federal exemption). But Massachusetts maintains a state estate tax with a much lower threshold. Without a credit-shelter trust to use the husband's state exemption at his death, his entire share of the marital estate flows to the wife (using the state-level marital deduction). At her later death, the entire combined estate is subject to Massachusetts estate tax with only her single state exemption available — Massachusetts does not recognize federal portability. Result: significant Massachusetts state estate-tax liability that a credit-shelter structure would have eliminated. The children inherit perhaps $300,000 less than they would have under appropriate state-level planning.

The federal exemption was identical for both couples. The outcome differed because of state-level rules and the presence (or absence) of credit-shelter planning. This is the texture of real exemption analysis.

What This Looks Like in Practice

Two married couples — Couple A in Florida, Couple B in Massachusetts — both with combined estates of approximately $4 million. Both husbands die first; both wives die four years later.

Couple A — Florida. Husband's death produces no federal tax (well below exemption) and no state tax (Florida has none). The executor still files Form 706 to elect portability, preserving the husband's unused federal exemption for the wife. The wife dies four years later with the combined estate (now $4.3 million after growth). Her estate is well below the doubled federal exemption. No federal tax. No Florida tax. The children inherit $4.3 million.

Couple B — Massachusetts. Husband's death produces no federal tax. Massachusetts maintains a state estate tax with a much lower threshold and does not recognize federal portability. Without a credit-shelter trust to use the husband's state exemption at his death, his entire share of the marital estate flows to the wife (using the state-level marital deduction). At her later death, the entire combined estate is subject to Massachusetts estate tax with only her single state exemption available. Result: significant state estate-tax liability that a credit-shelter structure would have eliminated.

Same federal exemption. Same family wealth. Different outcome, attributable entirely to the absence of state-level credit-shelter planning. The children inherit perhaps $300,000 less than they would have under appropriate state-level structuring.

Where We Go From Here

Notes on Practice

Portability is the most important planning election most families have not heard of. For married couples with potential federal exposure, a Form 706 election for portability on the first spouse's death is essentially free (it costs only the filing) and potentially saves millions of dollars in tax on the second spouse's death. The election must be timely. Missing it is a recurring source of regret.

A second observation: state-level credit-shelter trusts remain useful even with federal portability. Most state estate-tax regimes do not recognize federal portability. Married couples with state-level exposure should structure to use both spouses' state exemptions through bypass-trust planning.

Practitioner Patterns — Exemption Strategy

Three patterns recur in exemption-related planning.

First, the question of whether to use lifetime exemption now or preserve it for at-death use. The answer depends on expected appreciation. Lifetime exemption used now removes the asset and all future appreciation from the estate; exemption preserved for at-death use captures the asset at its date-of-death value. For highly appreciating assets with long expected hold periods, lifetime use is typically more valuable. For lower-appreciation assets and shorter horizons, at-death use captures the basis-step-up advantage discussed in Chapter 8.

Second, the use-it-or-lose-it concern around sunset provisions. The current high federal exemption is scheduled to sunset; estates that wait may face a substantially lower exemption at death. Many advisors recommend using lifetime exemption now (through sophisticated structures) for clients who would otherwise face exposure under post-sunset rules. The IRS has issued anti-clawback regulations confirming that lifetime exemption used at the current high level is not retroactively reduced after the sunset, making this a viable strategy for clients with appropriate facts.

Third, the credit-shelter trust resurgence. Federal portability reduced the need for credit-shelter trusts at the federal level. State-level estate taxes without state-level portability have preserved the need at the state level. For families in state-tax states, credit-shelter trusts remain essential. The trust funded at the first death with the deceased spouse's state exemption preserves both spouses' state exemptions across two deaths.

Portability Election Mechanics

Three details about the portability election deserve explicit treatment because each catches families in actual practice.

First, the timing requirement is strict. The Form 706 claiming portability must be filed within nine months of death, extendible to fifteen months on a timely Form 4768 extension request. After the deadline, portability is lost unless the IRS grants relief. The IRS has, in recent years, granted automatic relief in certain estates that timely elected on a late-filed return — but this relief is not universal and depends on facts. The safe approach is deliberate timely filing, not relief reliance.

Second, even no-tax estates should file. For a married couple where the first spouse to die has an estate well below the federal exemption, no estate tax is owed. But filing a Form 706 to elect portability — preserving the deceased spouse's unused exemption for the surviving spouse — is essentially free (cost of CPA filing) and potentially saves millions if the surviving spouse's eventual estate exceeds the surviving spouse's own exemption. The election is a one-way ratchet; not making it cannot be undone except through IRS relief procedures.

Third, portability does not affect the GST exemption. The deceased spouse's unused GST exemption is not portable. Married couples that wish to use both spouses' GST exemptions must do so through trust structures (typically a credit-shelter trust funded with the deceased spouse's GST exemption) rather than relying on portability. This is a live planning issue in practice.

Common Questions, Briefly

Should I elect portability if my surviving spouse remarries later?

Probably yes. Portability is determined by the most recently deceased spouse, but the unused exemption from the first spouse is preserved against the surviving spouse's own death even if the surviving spouse remarries — provided the new marriage does not result in a new spouse predeceasing. Counsel should review the specific facts; the rules are technical and the optimal strategy depends on family structure.

Can portability be used after the surviving spouse remarries and the new spouse dies?

Generally no, because the most-recently-deceased-spouse rule (§2010(c)(4)(B)) treats the new spouse as displacing the prior spouse for portability purposes. The surviving spouse can only use the unused exemption from the most recently deceased spouse. Some lifetime-use planning can preserve the first spouse's DSUE before the new spouse dies, but this is technical and requires specialist counsel.

Chapter 6 takes up the timing question: why the date-of-death valuation rule, the alternate valuation election, and the broader question of when ownership truly changed are more consequential than amount alone. Chapter 7 then treats the gift-tax interaction with estate tax, completing the integrated picture of the unified credit and the inclusion of adjusted taxable gifts in the estate-tax computation.

Figure 5.1

APPLICABLE EXCLUSION

Federal exemption per individual; indexed annually. Applies after inclusion.

CREDIT FORM

PORTABILITY (DSUE)

Surviving spouse uses unused exemption of deceased spouse. Election on Form 706 required.

DOUBLES COUPLE'S

STATE EXEMPTION

12 states + DC have lower thresholds than federal. Most don't honor portability.

STATE-SPECIFIC

UNIFIED CREDIT POOL

Same exemption covers gift and estate tax. Lifetime gifts reduce at-death amount.

SINGLE POOL

The federal exemption mechanism — applicable exclusion, portability, and the credit framework.

KEY POINT

The federal exemption is mechanically applied after inclusion is determined. Most of the interesting decisions are upstream of the exemption. State exemptions are much lower than federal and produce real exposure for many families that have no federal exposure.

What This Chapter Has Said

The federal exemption is structured as a credit applied after the rate computation. Portability effectively doubles it for married couples who timely elect. State exemption thresholds are typically much lower than federal. The exemption matters less than the inclusion question for most planning purposes.

PART IV

TIMING AND CONNECTIONS

Why timing matters more than amounts, and how the gift-tax system links to the estate-tax system.

CHAPTER 6

Why Timing Matters More Than Amounts

Chapter at a Glance

- The default date-of-death valuation rule and why it fixes tax at a single moment.
- The alternate valuation date election under §2032 — when it helps.
- Special use valuation under §2032A for qualifying farm and business real property.
- The deeper timing question — when ownership truly changed for tax purposes.
- Three planning implications: plan early, document carefully, watch the alternate valuation election.

Estate taxes are triggered by timing, not intention.

Control retained too long results in inclusion. Transfers completed too late fix higher values. Delays can collapse planning windows. Families often focus on how much something is worth. The system focuses on when ownership truly changed.

This is why timing errors cause more estate-tax surprises than valuation errors.

The Date-of-Death Valuation Rule

Internal Revenue Code section 2031 establishes the basic valuation rule: assets in the gross estate are valued at fair market value as of the date of the deceased's death. This is the default. It applies to every asset unless an alternate election is made (see below).

The date-of-death rule produces three practical consequences worth understanding.

First, valuation is fixed at a single point in time. The estate's tax exposure is determined by the value at death, regardless of subsequent appreciation or depreciation. A stock portfolio worth $10 million on the date of death remains $10 million for estate-tax purposes even if the market drops 20% the following month. The reverse is also true: an asset worth $5 million at death does not become $10 million for estate-tax purposes if the market rallies.

Second, the date-of-death valuation is also the basis for the recipient's eventual capital-gains tax (treated in Chapter 8). This dual function — both the tax base for estate tax and the basis for income-tax purposes — links the two systems and explains why valuation matters in two different directions simultaneously.

Third, the date is the date — not the date the executor discovered an asset, not the date probate opened, not the date a will was admitted. The valuation date is the moment of death. Assets discovered later are valued back to that moment.

The Alternate Valuation Date

Internal Revenue Code section 2032 permits the executor to elect, on a timely-filed Form 706, an alternate valuation date — a single date six months after the date of death. If elected, all assets in the gross estate are valued as of the alternate date rather than as of death.

The alternate-valuation election is available only when it produces both a lower gross estate AND a lower estate tax. The executor cannot cherry-pick — the election applies to all assets in the estate, not selected ones, and only if the overall result is lower tax.

The election is most often used in volatile markets when asset values have dropped meaningfully in the months following death — most prominently after the 2008 financial crisis, when many estates with date-of-death valuations in Q3 or Q4 of 2008 had alternate valuation dates falling in the first half of 2009 with substantially lower values. The election can save material tax in such circumstances. It must be made on the first-filed Form 706 and cannot be amended onto a later return.

Special Use Valuation — Section 2032A

A separate election under Internal Revenue Code section 2032A applies to qualified farm and closely held business real property. This election, where available, allows the property to be valued based on its actual use rather than its highest-and-best use. The reduction in includible value is capped (currently around $1.4 million, indexed) and comes with significant strings attached — including a ten-year recapture period during which the qualified use must continue.

Special use valuation is rare. It applies primarily to operating farms and family-controlled businesses with real-property components. Where it applies, it can meaningfully reduce gross estate. Where it does not apply, the standard date-of-death rule controls.

Timing of Transfers — When Ownership Actually Changed

The most consequential timing question in estate-tax practice is not the valuation date itself. It is the question of when ownership of an asset truly changed for tax purposes. The system's answer is sometimes different from the family's understanding, and the difference produces most of the inclusion surprises.

Consider three patterns:

(1) The signed deed that was never recorded. A parent signs a deed transferring property to a child during life but the deed is

never recorded. Some courts treat the unrecorded deed as effective between the parties (as a matter of property law) but ineffective against third parties (under the recording acts). The IRS's position can be that the transfer was not complete for federal tax purposes until the deed was actually recorded — meaning the property remained in the parent's gross estate at death even though the deed was signed years earlier.

(2) The trust funded with a future interest. A grantor establishes a trust during life with a complete transfer of property and a clearly stated future interest in the beneficiaries. Sections 2036 and 2037 ask whether the grantor retained any reversion or other reserved interest in the property. If so — even an unlikely contingent reversion — the trust assets may be includible in the grantor's gross estate at death. Timing of when the transfer was "complete for tax purposes" may differ from when the trust agreement was signed.

(3) The lifetime gift made too close to death. Most lifetime gifts are completely outside the gross estate, but section 2035's three-year lookback applies to specific categories — life-insurance transfers, transfers within sections 2036/2037/2038, and gift tax paid on transfers within three years of death. Families that wait too late to implement planning structures discover the lookback and lose the planning benefit.

> **KEY POINT**
>
> The estate-tax system asks two timing questions: when the deceased died (which fixes the valuation date), and when ownership of each asset truly changed for tax purposes (which fixes whether the asset is in the estate at all). The first is mechanical. The second is where most surprises live.

Planning Implications

Three planning implications follow from the timing rules.

(1) Plan early. Most timing-based inclusions arise because structures were implemented too late — within three years of death, or with the grantor's death intervening before the structure could ripen. Implementing early — meaning five or more years before any plausible death event — is the single most reliable cure for most timing-based inclusion.

(2) Document carefully. When ownership changes during life, document the change with appropriate instruments — recorded deeds, trust transfers with appropriate releases, beneficiary designations effective immediately, and contemporaneous documentation that the transfer was complete for property-law purposes. Sloppy documentation invites IRS challenge based on incomplete-transfer arguments.

(3) Watch the alternate valuation election. For estates filed in volatile market environments, the executor and CPA should specifically consider whether the alternate valuation date would produce lower tax. The election is made or lost on the first-filed Form 706 and cannot be added later.

What This Looks Like in Practice

A founder — call him David — built a closely held business over forty years. By his late seventies, the business was valued at approximately $20 million. David's estate planner suggested a transfer to a defective grantor trust (a sophisticated planning structure that, properly implemented, can move appreciating assets out of the estate while continuing to be taxed to the grantor for income-tax purposes — a useful asymmetry).

David delayed. The structure was implemented only when his health began to decline at age eighty-two — roughly two years before his death. Section 2035's three-year lookback applied to the life-insurance components of the structure. Section 2036 was asserted by the IRS as to the underlying business interests on the theory that David retained indirect control through his continued operating role. After audit, a meaningful portion of what was intended to be excluded was pulled back into the gross estate. The additional tax exceeded $4 million.

The structure was sound. The implementation was too late. David's estate paid the difference.

Most timing failures look like David's. The plan exists. The ink on the documents is old enough. But the underlying transfer was not complete for tax purposes early enough, or the wrong elements remained under the deceased's control, and the result is inclusion that careful early planning would have avoided.

What This Looks Like in Practice

A founder — call him David — built a closely held business over forty years. By his late seventies, the business was valued at approximately $20 million. David's estate planner suggested a transfer to a defective grantor trust (a sophisticated planning structure that, properly implemented, can move appreciating assets out of the estate while continuing to be taxed to the grantor for income-tax purposes — a useful asymmetry).

David delayed. The structure was implemented only when his health began to decline at age eighty-two — roughly two years before his death. Section 2035's three-year lookback applied to the life-insurance components of the structure. Section 2036 was asserted by the IRS as to the underlying business interests on the theory that David retained indirect control through his continued operating role. After audit, a meaningful portion of what was intended to be excluded was pulled back into the gross estate. The additional tax exceeded $4 million.

The structure was sound. The implementation was too late. David's estate paid the difference. Most timing failures look like David's. The plan exists. The ink on the documents is old enough. But the underlying transfer was not complete for tax purposes early enough, or the wrong elements remained under the deceased's control, and the result is inclusion that careful early planning would have avoided.

Where We Go From Here

Notes on Practice

The alternate valuation election under section 2032 is most often missed in volatile-market environments when it would have helped most. Estates filed shortly after a market decline routinely save substantial tax through the alternate valuation election if the executor and CPA are paying attention. The election must be made on the first-filed Form 706.

A second observation: timing-based inclusion (section 2036, the three-year lookback under section 2035) produces most of the planning failures we observe in actual practice. Implementing structures five or more years before death is the single most reliable cure. Planners working with clients in poor health should be candid about the limited planning options available with a short remaining horizon.

Practitioner Patterns — Timing Specific Strategies

Three timing-specific strategies deserve attention.

First, the QPRT (qualified personal residence trust) as a timing-driven structure. The donor transfers the residence to a trust for a term of years while retaining the right to occupy. At the end of the term, the residence passes to the remainder beneficiaries. The gift-tax cost is the present value of the remainder interest (much smaller than the home's full value). The strategy works only if the donor survives the term; if the donor dies during the term, the home is fully includible. QPRTs are useful in low-interest-rate environments for donors with strong likelihood of surviving the term.

Second, the GRAT (grantor retained annuity trust) as an appreciation-shifting structure. The donor transfers assets to a trust paying back a fixed annuity for a term of years; appreciation above the annuity rate (the §7520 rate) passes tax-free to remainder beneficiaries. The strategy works particularly well in low-rate environments and for highly appreciating assets. GRATs are widely used in sophisticated planning.

Third, the IDGT (intentionally defective grantor trust) as an income-tax-favorable structure. The trust is structured so that it is excluded from the donor's gross estate but is taxed to the donor for income-tax purposes (a deliberate "defect"). The donor pays income tax on trust earnings, effectively making additional tax-free transfers to the trust. Sophisticated structure; specialist guidance essential.

The Alternate Valuation Election in Practice

Two practical observations about the alternate valuation election (§2032) merit explicit treatment.

First, the election is all-or-nothing. The executor cannot elect alternate valuation for some assets and date-of-death valuation for others. The election applies to the entire gross estate. If overall the alternate date produces a lower estate tax (and a lower gross estate), the election is available; otherwise it is not. The CPA must compute the estate-tax outcome under both scenarios before making the election.

Second, the alternate valuation lowers basis. The basis-step-up under §1014 follows the value used for estate-tax purposes. If the alternate valuation date is elected, inheritors take a basis equal to the alternate-date value, not the date-of-death value. For estates in volatile markets, the alternate election may save estate tax but reduce future basis-step-up benefit. The trade-off depends on the family's expected sale horizon and the magnitude of the value change. Specialists model both scenarios explicitly.

Common Questions, Briefly

If property is sold during the six-month alternate-valuation period, what valuation applies?

The sale price applies. Under §2032, property disposed of during the six-month alternate-valuation window is valued at the disposition date and price, not at the original date-of-death or the six-month-later alternate date. This rule prevents executors from gaming the election by selectively timing dispositions.

Can the alternate valuation date be combined with the special use valuation under §2032A?

Yes, in principle. The two elections address different issues. The alternate valuation date moves the valuation date by six months; the special use valuation reduces the value of qualifying farm/business real property based on its current use. Both elections can be made on the same Form 706 if the estate qualifies. Specialist counsel is essential.

Chapter 7 takes up the gift-tax system and its connection to estate tax through the unified credit. Lifetime gifts interact with the at-death calculation in ways that often surprise families and that explain why the gift-tax system is best understood as the same system as the estate-tax system, not a separate one.

Figure 6.1

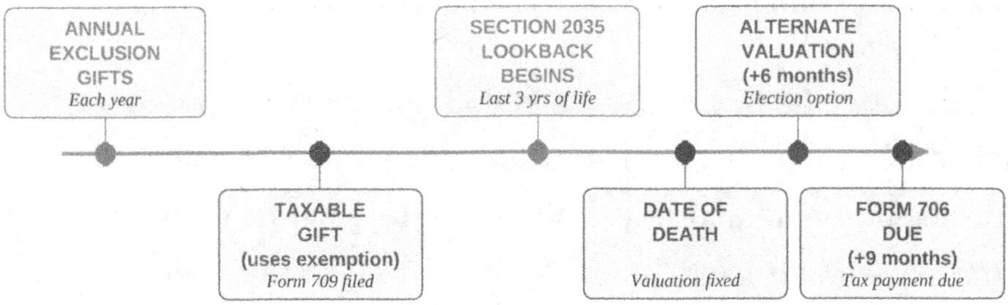

Timing across an estate's life — annual gifts, lookback windows, date of death, and filing deadlines.

KEY POINT

The estate-tax system asks two timing questions: when the deceased died (which fixes valuation), and when ownership truly changed (which fixes inclusion). The first is mechanical. The second is where most surprises live. Plan early.

What This Chapter Has Said

Estate-tax exposure is fixed at the date of death for valuation purposes. The alternate valuation date is available where it produces lower tax. Section 2035's three-year lookback applies to specific transfers. Plan early; document carefully; consider the alternate valuation election. Most timing failures arise from late implementation.

CHAPTER 7

Gift Taxes and Their Connection to Estate Taxes

Chapter at a Glance

- How gift tax and estate tax are coordinated through the unified credit.
- The four exclusions that allow most lifetime gifts without tax: annual exclusion, medical/educational, marital, charitable.
- Why filing Form 709 matters even when no gift tax is owed.
- Generation-skipping transfer (GST) tax — a separate parallel system with traps.
- Annual-exclusion gifting as the highest-leverage long-term estate-tax planning tool.

Estate taxes do not operate alone.

They are connected to gift taxes through a coordinated system that has been in place since the unification of the gift-tax and estate-tax credits in 1976. Transfers made during life and transfers made at death are tracked together. This prevents shifting assets earlier simply to avoid tax later.

Gift taxes are not penalties. They are balancing mechanisms. Understanding this connection explains why lifetime transfers still affect estate-tax outcomes.

The Federal Gift Tax in Outline

Internal Revenue Code Chapter 12 imposes a federal gift tax on transfers of property by gift during the donor's life. The tax is paid by the donor, not by the donee. Most lifetime gifts produce no actual tax because of three important exclusions and the unified credit:

(1) The annual exclusion. Under Internal Revenue Code section 2503(b), each donor may give up to a specified annual amount (currently around $19,000, indexed) per donee per year without using any lifetime exemption. Married couples can split gifts and effectively double the per-donee amount. Annual-exclusion gifts to as many donees as desired are entirely outside the transfer-tax system — they do not consume lifetime exemption and are not added back at death.

(2) The medical and educational exclusions. Section 2503(e) provides that direct payments to a medical provider for a person's medical expenses, and direct payments to an educational institution for a person's tuition, are entirely outside the gift-tax system regardless of amount. The payments must be made directly to the provider or institution, not to the recipient.

These exclusions are unlimited.

(3) The marital and charitable deductions. Gifts to a spouse who is a US citizen are unlimited and untaxed (section 2523, the gift-tax marital deduction). Gifts to qualified charities are unlimited and untaxed (section 2522). Both deductions parallel their estate-tax counterparts.

(4) The lifetime exemption. Above all of the above, each donor has a lifetime gift-tax exemption that runs concurrently with the estate-tax exemption — the unified credit. Lifetime gifts that exceed the annual exclusion and other exclusions consume lifetime exemption rather than producing tax, until the lifetime exemption is exhausted. Only after the lifetime exemption is fully used does the gift tax become a current cash-flow obligation.

The Unified Credit

The unified credit is the structural feature that links gift tax and estate tax. The same exemption pool covers both. A donor who uses, say, $5 million of lifetime exemption through gifts during life has $5 million less available at death. The estate-tax computation includes an "adjusted taxable gifts" addition that brings the lifetime gifts back into the estate-tax base for computational purposes — and the lifetime exemption used is then credited so that no double tax results.

The mechanics, simplified: at death, the executor computes the federal estate tax on the sum of (taxable estate + adjusted taxable gifts), applies the unified credit equal to the unused lifetime exemption, and reports the net tax on Form 706. If the deceased used substantial lifetime exemption, the unified credit at death is correspondingly smaller and more of the at-death wealth becomes subject to tax.

Table 7.1

Item	Effect on estate-tax computation
Annual-exclusion gifts ($19k/donee/yr indexed)	No effect — entirely outside the transfer-tax system.
Medical / educational direct payments (§2503(e))	No effect — entirely outside the system.
Marital gifts (US citizen spouse)	No effect — unlimited gift-tax marital deduction.
Charitable gifts to qualified charities	No effect — unlimited charitable deduction.
Lifetime gifts using exemption	Added back to estate-tax base ("adjusted taxable gifts"); exemption used reduces credit available at death.
Gift tax paid more than 3 years before death	Outside the gross estate — the tax paid is gone but reduces future tax exposure.
Gift tax paid within 3 years of death (§2035(b))	Added back to the gross estate ("gross-up").
Lifetime gift to GST skip person (grandchild)	May trigger generation-skipping transfer tax in addition to gift tax.

How lifetime gifts interact with the estate-tax computation.

When Gift Tax Actually Becomes Cash

Federal gift tax becomes a cash-flow event for the donor only when the donor's cumulative lifetime taxable gifts exceed the donor's available lifetime exemption. For most American families, this never happens — the lifetime exemption (currently many millions of dollars) is far above what most families gift over a lifetime.

Filing a gift-tax return (Form 709), however, is required for most non-annual-exclusion gifts even when no tax is owed. The return reports the gift, the value, and the use of lifetime exemption. The IRS uses these returns to track cumulative use of exemption across the donor's lifetime. Failure to file a required return preserves the IRS's ability to challenge the value of the gift indefinitely (the statute of limitations does not run on an unfiled return).

Counsel and CPAs routinely recommend filing Form 709 even for borderline cases — small business interests gifted with claimed valuation discounts, gifts to trusts, split-gift elections — to start the statute running and lock in the reported value.

The Generation-Skipping Transfer Tax

A separate federal tax — the generation-skipping transfer tax under Internal Revenue Code Chapter 13 — applies in addition to estate and gift taxes when a transfer skips a generation. The classic example: a grandparent transfers property to a grandchild, bypassing the parent. The transfer is subject to gift or estate tax in the ordinary way, AND, if it exceeds the GST exemption, to an additional flat-rate generation-skipping tax.

The GST exemption is a separate pool from the estate/gift exemption — though it is set at the same dollar level and indexed the same way. Each individual has a GST exemption that can be allocated to particular transfers. Allocating GST exemption is a technical exercise that requires specialist guidance; mishandled, the GST tax can produce an additional 40% federal tax on transfers that the family did not realize were exposed.

The two most common GST traps in ordinary family practice:

- Trusts established for grandchildren without adequate GST exemption allocation. The omitted allocation can produce GST tax on later distributions.
- Outright bequests to grandchildren when the parent (the deceased's child) is still alive. The bequest is a direct-skip transfer that consumes GST exemption.

Where GST exposure is meaningful, specialized counsel is essential. The traps are subtle and the cost of mistakes is high.

> **REFLECTION**
>
> The transfer-tax system tracks lifetime transfers and at-death transfers as a single integrated story. The exemption is a one-time allowance against the donor's transfers, whenever they occur. Treating gift tax and estate tax as separate systems leads to bad planning. Treating them as the same system leads to better outcomes.

Annual-Exclusion Gifting as a Long-Term Strategy

For families with potential federal estate-tax exposure, annual-exclusion gifting is the single most reliable long-term planning tool. The numbers compound:

- A married couple can gift roughly $38,000/year to each child, grandchild, child-in-law — currently — without using any lifetime exemption.
- Over twenty years, a couple with three children, three children-in-law, and six grandchildren can transfer approximately $9 million through annual-exclusion gifts alone (twelve donees × $38k × 20 years).
- These transfers are entirely outside the transfer-tax system. They consume no lifetime exemption. They are not added back at death. They reduce the eventual taxable estate dollar-for-dollar.
- The transfers can be made directly, through annual-exclusion trusts, through 529 college-savings plans,

or in kind (gift of stock, gift of partial property interests).

For families that engage with annual-exclusion gifting consistently over decades, the cumulative reduction in estate-tax exposure is substantial. For families that wait until late life to begin, the available years are fewer and the cumulative effect is smaller. Annual-exclusion gifting is, like compound interest, a long-horizon tool.

What This Looks Like in Practice

Two married couples with potential estate-tax exposure. Couple A starts annual-exclusion gifting in their early fifties; Couple B does not gift at all and discovers the exposure only at age seventy-five.

Couple A makes maximum annual-exclusion gifts to their three children and (eventually) seven grandchildren over a thirty-year period. Across that period, indexing increases the per-donee amount roughly in line with inflation. Cumulative gifts: approximately $14-16 million, depending on indexing and family composition over time. Lifetime exemption used: zero. The $14-16 million has been transferred entirely outside the transfer-tax system and is not in the couple's eventual estates at all.

Couple B has the same wealth at age seventy-five. They now have ten years of expected life remaining and can still annual-exclusion gift. With ten donees and ten years, they transfer approximately $4-5 million through annual-exclusion gifts. The remaining wealth — much larger than Couple A's — remains in their estates and is exposed to whatever estate-tax regime applies at their deaths.

Same starting wealth. Same family structure. Different engagement with the annual exclusion over time. The cumulative difference in estate-tax exposure is in the millions of dollars. This is what early gift-tax planning produces over a long horizon.

What This Looks Like in Practice

Two married couples with potential estate-tax exposure. Couple A starts annual-exclusion gifting in their early fifties; Couple B does not gift at all and discovers the exposure only at age seventy-five.

Couple A makes maximum annual-exclusion gifts to their three children and (eventually) seven grandchildren over a thirty-year period. Across that period, indexing increases the per-donee amount roughly in line with inflation. Cumulative gifts: approximately $14-16 million, depending on indexing and family composition over time. Lifetime exemption used: zero. The $14-16 million has been transferred entirely outside the transfer-tax system and is not in the couple's eventual estates at all.

Couple B has the same wealth at age seventy-five. They now have ten years of expected life remaining and can still annual-exclusion gift. With ten donees and ten years, they transfer approximately $4-5 million through annual-exclusion gifts. The remaining wealth — much larger than Couple A's — remains in their estates and is exposed to whatever estate-tax regime applies at their deaths.

Same starting wealth. Same family structure. Different engagement with the annual exclusion over time. The cumulative difference in estate-tax exposure is in the millions of dollars. This is what early gift-tax planning produces over a long horizon.

Where We Go From Here

Notes on Practice

Annual-exclusion gifting is the single most underused estate-tax planning tool. Many families who could comfortably gift $19k per donee per year do not, often because they have not had the conversation with counsel about whether such gifts would be useful. For families with potential federal exposure, even modest annual gifting over a long horizon dramatically reduces eventual tax. The conversation should happen early.

A second observation: GST allocation on Form 709 is a frequent area of CPA error. The default rules and the available elections are technical. Mishandled GST allocation can produce a 40% federal tax on transfers families did not realize were exposed. Where GST exposure is meaningful, specialist counsel is essential.

Practitioner Patterns — Gift Tax Subtleties

Three gift-tax patterns appear often enough to warrant explicit treatment.

First, gift splitting between spouses. Married couples can elect to treat gifts made by either spouse as made half by each — effectively doubling the per-donee annual exclusion. The election is made on Form 709 by both spouses. It applies to all gifts in the year (cannot be cherry-picked). Where one spouse has the assets and both want to use both annual exclusions, gift splitting is the mechanism.

Second, the Crummey power for trust gifts. Annual-exclusion treatment requires that the gift be of a present interest. Gifts to trusts (which generally give beneficiaries only future interests) ordinarily would not qualify. The Crummey power — giving the beneficiary a temporary right to withdraw the contribution — converts the gift to a present interest for annual-exclusion purposes. The power must be real (not merely formal) and notice must be given. Trust drafting must support the Crummey structure for ILITs and similar trusts.

Third, the §2503(c) trust for minors. A trust for a minor can qualify for annual-exclusion treatment if it permits use of income and principal for the minor's benefit and distributes to the minor at age 21 (or earlier). The structure permits annual-exclusion gifting to minors who cannot effectively exercise a Crummey power.

The Mathematics of Compounding Annual Exclusions

Annual-exclusion gifting has a deceptively simple mathematical structure that reveals its long-term power.

Consider a married couple with three children, three in-laws, and six grandchildren — twelve donees. At the current annual exclusion of approximately $19,000 per donee (indexed) and gift-splitting between the spouses ($38,000 per donee per year combined), the couple can transfer $456,000 per year through annual-exclusion gifts alone. These transfers consume no lifetime exemption.

Over twenty years (roughly the late-fifties through mid-seventies for many planners), with modest indexing of the annual-exclusion amount, the cumulative transfers approach $10 million. The transfers are entirely outside the transfer-tax system — no estate tax, no gift tax, no GST tax (within proper structures), no use of lifetime exemption. The donees can receive the transfers in cash, in shares of stock, in interests in family entities, or in 529 college-savings accounts.

The compound effect goes further. If the gifted assets appreciate at typical investment rates, the donees' assets grow tax-free for transfer-tax purposes (subject to their own income-tax obligations). Twenty years of annual-exclusion gifting plus appreciation on the gifted assets can result in tens of millions of dollars of family wealth transferred outside the transfer-tax system entirely. For families with potential federal estate-tax exposure, this is the single most reliable long-term planning tool.

GST Allocation in Practice

Generation-skipping transfer tax allocation is more technical than ordinary practice usually suggests. The default rules under §2632 automatically allocate GST exemption to certain transfers ("indirect skips") unless the donor affirmatively elects out. The default rules are not always optimal. Three patterns in practice:

(1) Trusts established for grandchildren without timely allocation. The default rules may automatically allocate GST exemption to such trusts, which can be appropriate. But families that fail to file Form 709 for the gift may discover that the automatic allocation did not occur as expected — and that GST tax now applies to subsequent distributions.

(2) The election out for transfers to non-skip trusts. Some transfers to trusts that have skip-person beneficiaries are automatically allocated GST exemption. Where the transfer is intended primarily for non-skip beneficiaries (children rather than grandchildren), electing out of automatic allocation

preserves the GST exemption for other uses.

(3) Late allocation and the Treasury relief procedures. Families that have failed to allocate GST exemption appropriately can sometimes obtain relief through the 9100 relief procedures, which permit late allocation in appropriate cases. The relief is not automatic; the IRS evaluates whether the late allocation is appropriate under the facts.

Common Questions, Briefly

Can I make a gift to my child's college savings account that exceeds the annual exclusion?

Yes, with the §529 "superfunding" election. Section 529(c)(2)(B) permits a single contribution of up to five times the annual exclusion (currently $95,000 per donee) to be treated as having been made ratably over five years for annual-exclusion purposes. This permits a substantial front-loaded contribution while still using only annual exclusion. The election is made on Form 709. Particularly useful for grandparents wishing to fully fund a grandchild's education savings.

Are gifts to a spouse subject to gift tax?

No, for gifts to a US citizen spouse — the unlimited gift-tax marital deduction (§2523) covers these transfers without tax or use of exemption. For gifts to a non-citizen spouse, a special annual exclusion (currently around $185,000, indexed) applies; transfers above that amount use lifetime exemption or produce gift tax.

Part V (Chapters 8 and 9) takes up the basis-step-up rules and the income-tax consequences of inheritance. Where the transfer taxes (estate, gift, GST) determine what gets transferred without tax, the basis rules determine the income-tax consequences when inherited property is later sold. For most American families, the basis-step-up matters more than any of the transfer taxes — and the planning interactions between basis and transfer tax are the single most consequential planning area.

Figure 7.1

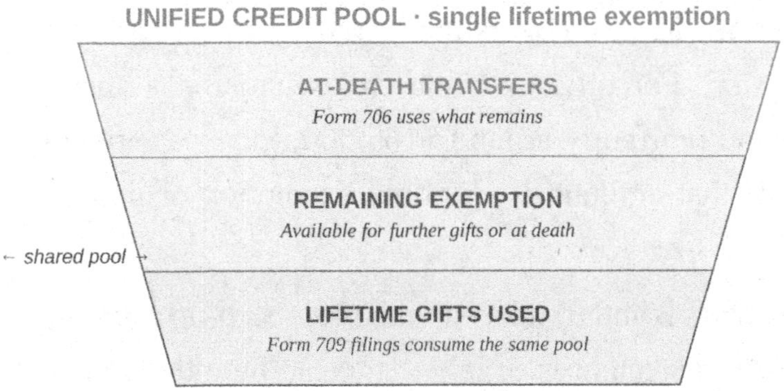

The unified credit — a single shared pool that covers both lifetime gifts and at-death transfers.

> **KEY POINT**
>
> Gift tax and estate tax are two parts of a single coordinated system. Annual-exclusion gifting, properly executed over a long horizon, is the highest-leverage long-term planning tool available to families with potential estate-tax exposure.

What This Chapter Has Said

Lifetime gifts and at-death transfers are tracked together through the unified credit. Annual-exclusion gifts, medical and educational direct payments, marital gifts, and charitable gifts are entirely outside the transfer-tax system. Filing Form 709 matters even when no tax is owed. GST tax is a separate parallel system. Annual-exclusion gifting over a long horizon dramatically reduces eventual estate-tax exposure.

PART V

◆

BASIS AND CAPITAL GAINS

Why basis matters more than estate tax for most families — and what the step-up at death actually does.

CHAPTER 8

Basis and the Step-Up Explained Simply

Chapter at a Glance

- What basis is and how it determines capital gain on eventual sale.
- How the basis step-up under §1014 works — and why it eliminates pre-death appreciation.
- The community-property double step-up advantage.
- What does and does not receive a step-up — IRAs, IRD, and irrevocable-trust property excluded.
- The basis-step-up versus estate-tax trade-off, and the common amateur mistake of gifting appreciated property during life.

One of the most misunderstood tax concepts at death is basis.

Basis determines capital gains. When someone dies, many assets receive a step-up in basis, resetting their value for tax purposes. This can eliminate large capital gains that would otherwise be owed if the asset were sold.

This rule often matters more financially than estate taxes themselves.

Families who misunderstand basis frequently make poor decisions after death — selling at the wrong time, holding for the wrong reasons, gifting appreciated property during life when inheritance would have been radically more favorable. Understanding basis is, for most American families, the single most important tax concept in this entire book.

What Basis Actually Is

Basis is the tax-significant cost of an asset. When the asset is sold, the difference between the sale price and the basis is the gain (or loss) for income-tax purposes. Capital-gains tax is computed on that gain.

Basis comes from one of three principal sources:

- Purchase basis — what the owner paid for the asset, plus any subsequent improvements.
- Carryover basis — for assets received as a gift, the donor's original basis carries over to the donee (Internal Revenue Code section 1015).
- Stepped-up basis — for assets received from a deceased person, the basis is reset to the fair market value at the date of death (or alternate valuation date), under Internal Revenue Code section 1014.

The basis-step-up at death is one of the most generous provisions in the entire Internal Revenue Code. It eliminates, in a single moment, all the unrealized appreciation that accrued during the deceased's lifetime. For long-term homeowners, long-term stock investors, and any family with substantially appreciated property, the basis-step-up is the most valuable tax provision they will ever encounter.

How the Step-Up Works

Internal Revenue Code section 1014 provides that when an individual inherits property from a deceased person, the individual's basis in that property is the fair market value as of the date of the deceased's death (or, if the alternate valuation date is elected, that date). The deceased's original basis is discarded. The accumulated appreciation, no matter how large, becomes invisible to the income-tax system.

Consider a parent who bought a house in 1985 for $80,000, lived in it for forty years, and dies in 2026 with the house worth $720,000 at the date of death. Under basis carryover rules (which would apply if the parent had gifted the house during life), the donee child would take a $80,000 basis and owe capital-gains tax on $640,000 of appreciation when the house was eventually sold. Under basis step-up rules (which apply when the child inherits at death), the child takes a $720,000 basis. If the child sells immediately for $720,000, no gain is recognized. The full $640,000 of lifetime appreciation is forgiven for income-tax purposes.

At a 23.8% combined long-term capital-gains and net-investment-income tax rate (federal), the basis-step-up saves roughly $152,000 in tax in this example. At higher state-level rates (California's combined federal-plus-state long-term capital-gains rate exceeds 33%), the savings are larger. For long-held property, the basis-step-up routinely saves families hundreds of thousands of dollars in income tax.

Table 8.1

Transfer mechanism	Basis to recipient	Tax consequence
Inherited at death (sole owner)	FMV at date of death (§1014)	Pre-death appreciation forgiven.
Inherited at death (revocable trust)	FMV at date of death	Same — revocable trust does not change result.
Surviving joint tenant (non-spouse)	Half stepped up; survivor's half retains carryover	Half of pre-death appreciation forgiven.
Surviving joint tenant (spouse, non-CP state)	Half stepped up; survivor's half retains original	Half of pre-death appreciation forgiven.
Surviving spouse (community property)	Both halves stepped up to FMV at first death	All pre-death appreciation forgiven.
Lifetime gift to child	Carryover (donor's original basis, §1015)	Pre-gift appreciation taxed to donee on later sale.
Quitclaim into revocable trust during life	No change (settlor still treated as owner)	No income-tax effect during life.
Sale to family member at FMV	Buyer's purchase price	Pre-sale appreciation taxed to seller.
Inherited by surviving CPWROS election	Both halves stepped up, automatic transfer	All pre-death appreciation forgiven (and no probate).

Basis treatment under various transfer scenarios.

The Community-Property Advantage

The single most favorable basis treatment under American tax law is the double basis step-up available to surviving spouses in community-property states. Under Internal Revenue Code section 1014(b)(6), both the deceased spouse's half AND the surviving spouse's half of community property are treated as receiving a basis step-up at the first spouse's death.

This is dramatically more favorable than the half step-up produced by joint tenancy in non-community-property states, in which only the deceased's half is stepped up.

Spouses moving from a community-property state to a non-community-property state should consult counsel before retitling marital real estate in joint tenancy with right of survivorship — joint titling can inadvertently sacrifice the double basis step-up that the original community-property treatment would have preserved.

What Does and Does Not Receive the Step-Up

Most assets received from a decedent receive the basis step-up. A short list of important exceptions:

- Retirement accounts (IRAs, 401(k)s) do NOT receive a basis step-up. The beneficiary takes over the deceased's pre-tax balance and pays income tax on distributions in the ordinary way.

- Annuities do NOT receive a basis step-up on the income portion.
- Income in respect of a decedent (IRD) — earned but uncollected income at death — does NOT receive a step-up. The beneficiary pays income tax on receipt as the deceased would have.
- Property held in a typical irrevocable trust funded during the decedent's lifetime may NOT receive the step-up if the property was excluded from the gross estate (the asymmetry: exclusion from estate tax often comes with no step-up).

These exceptions matter for planning. The retirement account in particular catches families off guard — the IRA inherited from a parent generates ordinary-income tax on every distribution, whereas the brokerage account inherited from the same parent generates only post-step-up capital gain on sale. Two assets of equal date-of-death value can produce very different after-tax results for the heir.

The Basis-Step-Up Versus Estate Tax Trade-Off

For families with potential federal estate-tax exposure, a subtle but important planning trade-off arises between removing assets from the estate (to avoid 40% estate tax) and keeping them in the estate (to obtain the basis step-up).

The trade-off depends on the asset's appreciation potential and the family's expected sale horizon:

- Highly appreciating assets that the family expects to sell soon after death: the basis-step-up is more valuable than estate-tax exclusion. Keep the asset in the estate.
- Highly appreciating assets that the family expects to hold for decades: estate-tax exclusion may be more valuable than basis-step-up, depending on the assumed appreciation rate and the family's eventual sale horizon. Remove the asset from the estate via lifetime gift or trust transfer.
- Slowly appreciating or depreciating assets that the family expects to sell soon: the basis-step-up is less valuable; estate-tax exclusion may dominate.
- Assets with low or zero unrealized appreciation: no step-up benefit; the analysis is purely estate-tax.

This trade-off is the core of sophisticated estate-tax planning. Specialists model it explicitly using assumed appreciation rates, holding periods, and tax rates. For ordinary families with no federal estate-tax exposure, the trade-off is moot — the basis-step-up is purely positive, with no offsetting cost — and lifetime gifting of appreciated property is almost always the wrong move.

> **KEY POINT**
>
> For most American families, the basis-step-up at death matters more financially than the estate tax. Lifetime gifting of appreciated property loses the step-up and produces income-tax consequences that often exceed the estate-tax savings the gift was meant to achieve. The first question in any planning conversation should be: would this asset receive a step-up at death, and how much capital-gains tax would the step-up save?

Why This Rule Often Matters More Than Estate Tax

Consider the populations affected by each rule.

The federal estate tax, in current form, applies to a small minority of American deaths — perhaps 0.1 to 0.2 percent. State estate and inheritance taxes affect a broader but still minority population. Most American families pay no transfer tax of any kind.

The basis-step-up rule, by contrast, applies to virtually every American family that owns appreciated property — which is to say, virtually every American homeowner, every American with a brokerage account, every American who has held an asset for more than a few years. The basis-step-up is a near-universal benefit, not a narrow one.

Families who misunderstand this often "plan" by gifting appreciated property to children during life on the theory that lifetime gifts reduce eventual estate tax. For most families, this is exactly backwards. The lifetime gift loses the basis-step-up and produces an income-tax obligation that the family would not have faced if the asset had been inherited at death. The "saved" estate tax is zero (because no estate tax would have applied anyway). The cost is the entire post-gift capital-gains exposure.

This is the single most common avoidable mistake in ordinary American estate planning. The cure is understanding the basis rule before any gift of appreciated property is made.

What This Looks Like in Practice

Consider three siblings — Anna, Brian, and Carl — whose father died with three principal assets: a primary residence purchased in 1985 ($80k basis, $720k value), an IRA balance ($400k), and a brokerage account ($600k basis low, $1.2m value).

The siblings inherit equal thirds of each asset. The basis treatment of each is sharply different.

The primary residence: each sibling takes a basis of $240k (one-third of the $720k stepped-up basis). They sell the residence within six months for $720k. No capital-gains tax owed. Net to each sibling: $240k cash.

The brokerage account: each sibling takes a basis of $400k (one-third of the $1.2m stepped-up basis). The full pre-death appreciation of $600k is forgiven. They liquidate the account at $1.2m. No capital-gains tax owed. Net to each sibling: $400k cash.

The IRA: each sibling takes a one-third interest in the $400k pre-tax balance. Distributions over time are taxable as ordinary income. The total income-tax cost to each sibling, depending on bracket and timing of distributions, may run $30,000 to $50,000 over the next ten years. Net after tax to each sibling: roughly $90k-$110k.

Same family. Same one-third interest in each asset. Sharply different after-tax results because of the basis treatment. Understanding the difference would let the siblings plan their distributions, choose which asset to spend down first (the one with the unfavorable tax treatment), and use the proceeds appropriately. Not understanding the difference produces preventable tax expense.

What This Looks Like in Practice

Three siblings — Anna, Brian, and Carl — whose father died with three principal assets: a primary residence purchased in 1985 ($80k basis, $720k value), an IRA balance ($400k), and a brokerage account ($600k basis low, $1.2m value).

The siblings inherit equal thirds of each asset. The basis treatment of each is sharply different.

The primary residence: each sibling takes a basis of $240k (one-third of the $720k stepped-up basis). They sell the residence within six months for $720k. No capital-gains tax owed. Net to each sibling: $240k cash.

The brokerage account: each sibling takes a basis of $400k (one-third of the $1.2m stepped-up basis). The full pre-death appreciation of $600k is forgiven. They liquidate the account at $1.2m. No capital-gains tax owed. Net to each sibling: $400k cash.

The IRA: each sibling takes a one-third interest in the $400k pre-tax balance. Distributions over time are taxable as ordinary income. The total income-tax cost to each sibling, depending on bracket and timing of distributions, may run $30,000 to $50,000 over the next ten years. Net after tax to each sibling: roughly $90k–$110k.

Same family. Same one-third interest in each asset. Sharply different after-tax results because of the basis treatment. Understanding the difference would let the siblings plan their distributions, choose which asset to spend down first, and use the proceeds appropriately. Not understanding the difference produces preventable tax expense.

Where We Go From Here

Notes on Practice

Lifetime gifting of appreciated property to children is the single most common amateur planning mistake we observe. The donor loses the basis-step-up. The donee inherits the donor's original basis (often very low) and faces material capital-gains tax on eventual sale. For most families, the income-tax cost exceeds any estate-tax savings — sometimes by a wide margin. Counsel and CPAs should specifically ask, at the start of any planning conversation: "Are you thinking about giving appreciated assets to your children during life?" If yes, the conversation needs to address the basis trade-off before any gift is made.

A second observation: documenting date-of-death basis with a contemporaneous appraisal is essential. Reconstructing basis decades later is expensive and uncertain. The appraisal should be obtained within 90 days of death and retained permanently as part of the heir's tax records.

Practitioner Patterns — Basis Optimization

Three basis-optimization patterns are worth explicit treatment.

First, the upstream-gift strategy. For families with highly appreciated assets and elderly parents below the federal exemption, gifting the appreciated asset to the parent during life can produce a basis step-up at the parent's eventual death — assuming the gift is real, the parent retains the asset, and the parent does not receive the asset back during life (which would make the gift illusory under general anti-abuse principles). The strategy requires careful execution and independent counsel for the parent.

Second, the basis-stripping structure that doesn't work. Various promoters have over the years advertised structures supposedly producing basis step-up without estate inclusion. These structures do not work; they are inconsistent with the basic structure of §1014. Basis-step-up is available for property included in the gross estate. Property excluded from the gross estate does not receive a step-up. The two are linked and cannot be decoupled. Families should be wary of any promoter claiming otherwise.

Third, the community-property advantage for movers. Spouses moving from a community-property state (California, Texas, etc.) to a non-community-property state should consult counsel about community-property agreements that preserve community-property treatment for tax purposes. Without such an agreement, the move may inadvertently sacrifice the double basis step-up that the original community-property treatment would have preserved.

Carryover Basis Math — When Lifetime Gifting Costs More Than It Saves

The arithmetic of lifetime gifting versus inheritance is worth working out explicitly because it is the single most consequential planning question for many American families.

Consider a parent with a primary residence purchased forty years ago for $80,000. The home is currently worth $1,200,000. The parent's overall estate is $4 million — well below the federal exemption. The parent is considering gifting the home to a child during life.

Lifetime gift scenario: the child takes the parent's carryover basis of $80,000 (§1015). When the child later sells the home for $1,200,000 (assuming the same value at sale), the child realizes a $1,120,000 capital gain. At a combined federal-and-state long-term capital-gains rate of approximately 28% (federal LTCG plus NIIT plus typical state rate), the child owes approximately $313,000 of capital-gains tax. After tax, the child receives $887,000 from the sale.

Inheritance scenario: the parent retains the home; child inherits at the parent's death. Child's basis is $1,200,000 (the date-of-death FMV under §1014). Child sells the home shortly thereafter for $1,200,000 (assuming the same value). Child realizes zero gain. No capital-gains tax owed. Child receives the full $1,200,000 from the sale.

The federal estate tax saved by the lifetime gift: zero (the parent's estate was below the exemption). The income tax cost imposed by the lifetime gift: $313,000. Net family loss from the lifetime gift: $313,000.

This is the single most common amateur planning mistake we observe. Families gift appreciated property to children during life on the theory that lifetime gifts reduce eventual estate tax — without realizing that for most families with no federal exposure, the lifetime gift destroys hundreds of thousands of dollars of basis-step-up value. The cure is to ask the question explicitly before any gift of appreciated property is made.

Common Questions, Briefly

If I inherit property and rent it out, how does basis work?

Your basis is the date-of-death FMV. As you take depreciation deductions on the rental, your basis is reduced by the depreciation taken. When you eventually sell, your gain is computed against the depreciation-reduced basis. Depreciation recapture (a portion of gain taxed as ordinary income up to the cumulative depreciation) may apply on sale. The Section 121 exclusion does not apply to rental property unless it is converted to primary residence (with the 2-of-5-year rule).

What if the inherited property has lost value since the date of death — is there a loss to claim?

Yes, in principle. Inherited property held for personal use (the inheritor lives in it) does not produce a deductible loss on sale because personal-use losses are non-deductible. Inherited property held for investment or rental use can produce a deductible capital loss on sale at less than the stepped-up basis. The loss can offset other capital gains and (limited) ordinary income. Holding-period and use rules matter; consult tax counsel.

Chapter 9 takes up capital-gains tax in more detail — when it applies, when it does not, how it interacts with estate tax, and why understanding the interaction often matters more than understanding either tax in isolation.

Figure 8.1

Sample case: home with $80,000 basis, $720,000 fair market value

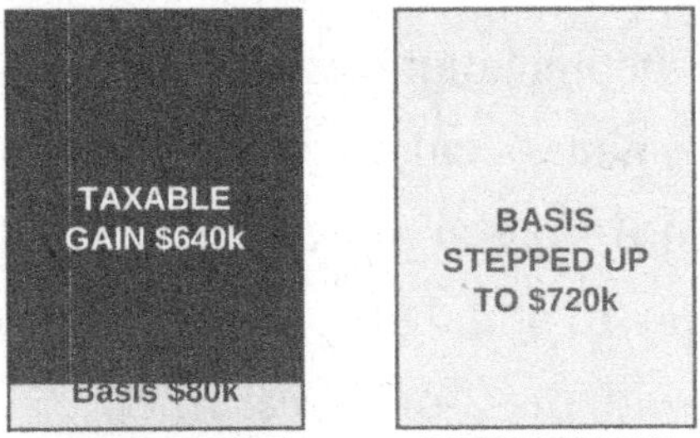

LIFETIME GIFT — *carryover basis*

INHERITANCE — *IRC §1014 step-up*

→ ~$96k–$152k tax savings ←

Lifetime gift vs. inheritance — the basis step-up at death eliminates pre-death appreciation from the income-tax base.

KEY POINT

For most American families, the basis-step-up at death matters more financially than the estate tax. Lifetime gifting of appreciated property loses the step-up. The first question in any planning conversation should be about basis, not exemption.

What This Chapter Has Said

The basis-step-up rule of IRC §1014 resets the basis of inherited property to fair market value at the date of death. This rule applies to most inherited property but not to retirement accounts or income in respect of a decedent. Joint property with non-spouses receives only a half step-up. Community-property states receive a particularly favorable double step-up. The basis-step-up is, for most families, more financially significant than the estate tax itself.

CHAPTER 9

Capital Gains After Death

Chapter at a Glance

- Why capital-gains tax applies on sale, not on inheritance.
- Inherited property's automatic long-term holding-period treatment.
- When capital gains apply, when they do not, and how to distinguish ordinary income from capital gain.
- The Section 121 home-sale exclusion ($250k single / $500k joint).
- Three planning rules of thumb: sell soon, document basis, expect only half step-up for joint-with-non-spouse.

Capital gains tax is different from estate tax.

It applies when assets are sold, not when they are inherited. Understanding when capital gains apply — and when they do not — prevents unnecessary fear and bad timing decisions.

Estate taxes and capital gains taxes interact, but they are not the same thing.

What Capital-Gains Tax Is

Capital-gains tax is an income tax imposed on the gain realized when a capital asset is sold for more than its tax basis. The applicable rates depend on the holding period and the seller's overall income.

For long-term capital gains (assets held more than one year), the federal rate structure is preferential:

- 0% for taxpayers in the lower income brackets
- 15% for most taxpayers in the middle brackets
- 20% for high-income taxpayers (above specified thresholds)
- Plus a 3.8% Net Investment Income Tax (NIIT) for taxpayers above further thresholds

For short-term capital gains (assets held one year or less), the gain is taxed as ordinary income at the taxpayer's marginal rate — up to 37% federally, plus state.

The state-level treatment of capital gains varies. Most states tax capital gains as ordinary income; a few (notably California) impose particularly high state rates that, combined with federal, can push the total long-term capital-gains rate above 33%.

Inherited Assets and the Long-Term Holding Rule

Internal Revenue Code section 1223(9) provides that inherited property is automatically treated as held for more than one year for capital-gains purposes — meaning any gain on sale qualifies for the favorable long-term rates regardless of how briefly the inheritor held the property.

This rule complements the basis-step-up. An inheritor who sells inherited property the day after the deceased's death pays long-term rates (preferential) on the gain (which is small, because of the basis-step-up). The combination of favorable basis and favorable holding period makes inherited property unusually advantageous for the recipient who sells soon after inheritance.

When Capital-Gains Tax Applies (and When It Does Not)

Several common scenarios are worth distinguishing because families consistently confuse them.

Table 9.1

Event	Capital-gains tax?	Notes
Inheriting property from a deceased person	No	Inheritance itself is not a sale event.
Selling inherited property at FMV at date of death	No (essentially)	Sale price ≈ basis; gain is roughly zero.
Selling inherited property a year later for higher price	Yes — on appreciation post-inheritance	Gain is sale price minus stepped-up basis.
Selling inherited property for less than date-of-death value	No (loss may be deductible)	Loss may offset gains or, limited, ordinary income.
Inheriting an IRA and taking distributions	Ordinary income tax (not capital-gains)	IRAs do not receive basis step-up; distributions are ordinary income.
Inheriting a residence and continuing to live in it	No (no sale event)	Use of property is not a taxable event.
Inheriting property and renting it out	Rental income taxed as ordinary income; sale taxed when realized	Rental converts the asset to investment property; depreciation may apply.
Receiving life insurance proceeds	No	Life insurance proceeds are generally income-tax-free.
Inheriting a primary residence; selling after living in it 2+ years	Possible §121 exclusion ($250k single / $500k joint)	If used as primary residence for 2 of last 5 years before sale.

When capital-gains tax applies — common inheritance scenarios.

The Section 121 Home-Sale Exclusion

Internal Revenue Code section 121 provides a separate, powerful exclusion for the sale of a principal residence: single taxpayers may exclude up to $250,000 of capital gain on the sale of their primary residence; married couples filing jointly may exclude up to $500,000. The exclusion applies if the taxpayer owned and used the property as a primary residence for at least two of the five years preceding the sale.

For inheritors who eventually convert an inherited property to their own primary residence, the section 121 exclusion stacks with the basis step-up — meaning that even post-inheritance appreciation can be excluded if the inheritor lives in the property for two years before selling. This is one of the most generous combined treatments in the entire Code.

For inheritors who simply hold and sell inherited property without occupancy, the section 121 exclusion does not apply (it requires the seller's own ownership and use). But the basis step-up alone usually eliminates most of the gain anyway, especially if the sale occurs within a year or two of inheritance.

Capital-Gains Planning for Inherited Property

Three planning rules of thumb apply to most inherited-property situations:

(1) Sell within the first year if a sale is the eventual plan. Holding inherited property for years before selling creates

post-inheritance appreciation that is taxable. Selling soon captures the basis-step-up most cleanly. The long-term holding rule means the rate is favorable even for quick sales.

(2) Document the date-of-death basis. The basis-step-up is documentary — it depends on a defensible appraisal of the property's fair market value as of the date of the deceased's death. A formal appraisal obtained within the first ninety days, and retained permanently, is the evidentiary backbone of any future sale. Reconstructing basis years later is materially harder and more expensive.

(3) For property held jointly with non-spouses, expect only a half step-up. Joint tenancy with adult children produces only a partial step-up at the parent's death. The child's existing half retains its (typically zero) carryover basis. This is one of several reasons joint titling with adult children for probate-avoidance purposes is usually a poor planning move.

REFLECTION

Capital-gains tax on inherited property is, for most families, a smaller worry than they fear. The basis-step-up is generous. The long-term holding rule is favorable. The section 121 exclusion adds further protection for inheritors who choose to live in the property. The combination is one of the most taxpayer-friendly arrangements in American income-tax law.

What This Looks Like in Practice

A daughter inherits her mother's primary residence. The mother bought the home in 1992 for $180,000. The home is worth $1.1 million at the date of death. The daughter is unsure whether to sell, hold, or move in.

Selling immediately: basis steps up to $1.1 million. Sale at $1.1 million produces zero gain. No federal or state capital-gains tax. Net to daughter: $1.1 million minus selling costs.

Holding for ten years (rented out): basis is $1.1 million; depreciation reduces basis over time; appreciation during the ten years is taxable on eventual sale. If the home appreciates to $1.6 million by sale and the daughter has taken $200,000 of depreciation, taxable gain is approximately $700,000. Combined federal and state capital-gains tax could exceed $200,000.

Moving in and selling after two years: basis is $1.1 million plus any post-inheritance appreciation. With the Section 121 exclusion, the entire post-inheritance appreciation may be excluded. Effective federal tax: zero.

Same starting position. Three different post-inheritance holding strategies. Sharply different after-tax outcomes. The decision matters.

Where We Go From Here

Notes on Practice

The Section 121 home-sale exclusion is one of the most generous combined provisions in the entire Internal Revenue Code, but it requires planning. Inheritors who intend to sell an inherited residence should consider whether a brief period of personal occupancy could qualify them for the exclusion, which stacks with the basis-step-up. The two-of-five-year ownership-and-use rule is precise; occupancy that almost satisfies it does not.

A second observation: capital-gains tax on inherited property is, for most families, smaller than they fear. The combination of basis-step-up, automatic long-term holding-period treatment, and (for occupants) the section 121 exclusion produces favorable outcomes. Counsel and CPAs should be willing to share this reassurance early.

Practitioner Patterns — Capital-Gains Coordination

Three coordination patterns between capital-gains and estate-tax planning are worth attention.

First, the swap-and-sell strategy. A donor who has transferred appreciated assets to a grantor trust during life can, before death, swap higher-basis assets back into the trust in exchange for the appreciated low-basis assets. The swap is not a taxable event for grantor-trust purposes. The donor then dies holding the low-basis assets, which receive the basis-step-up. The trust holds the higher-basis assets, which it sells without the step-up but with less embedded gain. The strategy is technical and requires close monitoring of valuation; it works only when executed properly.

Second, the deferral-of-gain strategy. Some inheritors hold inherited property longer than would otherwise be optimal because they (incorrectly) believe that holding longer reduces tax. With the basis-step-up, holding longer actually increases tax exposure (post-death appreciation is taxable). Selling soon after inheritance is usually optimal for tax-minimization purposes.

Third, the §1031 exchange after inheritance. Real property received by inheritance can be exchanged for like-kind property under §1031 to defer recognition of any post-inheritance gain. The basis carries over to the replacement property. The strategy is useful for inheritors who want to redeploy real-estate holdings while deferring tax on any post-inheritance appreciation.

The Net Investment Income Tax (NIIT)

A subtle but consequential additional tax on capital gains deserves explicit treatment. Under Internal Revenue Code §1411, an additional 3.8% Net Investment Income Tax (NIIT) applies to net investment income (including most capital gains) for taxpayers above specified income thresholds. The NIIT applies on top of long-term capital-gains rates.

The thresholds (which were not indexed for inflation when enacted in 2010 and have eroded in real terms since): $250,000 of modified adjusted gross income for married filing jointly, $200,000 for single filers, $125,000 for married filing separately. Above these thresholds, the 3.8% NIIT applies to the lesser of net investment income or modified AGI in excess of the threshold.

For estates and certain trusts, a separate NIIT analysis applies. The thresholds for trusts and estates are much lower (currently around $14,450, the threshold for the highest trust income-tax bracket). Estates that retain investment income during administration face NIIT exposure above the low threshold; distributing income to beneficiaries (who have higher individual thresholds) may produce a more favorable overall result.

Common Questions, Briefly

Does the basis-step-up apply to property held in a revocable living trust?

Yes. Property in a revocable living trust at the grantor's death receives the basis-step-up under §1014, just like property held in the grantor's individual name. The trust's revocability means the grantor was treated as the owner for income-tax purposes during life; the death triggers the step-up. Successor trustees should obtain date-of-death appraisals for trust property.

What if the deceased held appreciated property in joint tenancy with a non-spouse?

Half step-up. The deceased's half receives a basis step-up to date-of-death FMV (the deceased's half is included in the gross estate under §2040). The surviving co-tenant's half retains its original basis (the survivor's contribution did not produce inclusion and does not produce step-up). This is one of several reasons joint tenancy with adult children is usually a poor planning structure for appreciated property.

Part VI takes up the question we have been circling throughout the book: why families get surprised by estate taxes despite all of the above being knowable in advance, and what the patterns of surprise actually look like in real practice. Chapter 10 catalogs the recurring surprises and points readers toward the specific planning moves that prevent each one.

Figure 9.1

Capital-gains treatment after death — three sale scenarios for inherited property.

KEY POINT

Capital-gains tax on inherited property is, for most families, smaller than feared. The basis-step-up is generous, the long-term holding rule is favorable, and the Section 121 exclusion stacks for inheritors who occupy.

What This Chapter Has Said

Capital-gains tax applies on sale, not on inheritance. Inherited property is automatically long-term-held for rate purposes. With the basis-step-up, gain on prompt post-inheritance sale is usually zero. Section 121 provides further exclusion for inheritors who occupy and sell. Sell soon if a sale is the eventual plan; document the date-of-death basis; expect only a half step-up for joint property with non-spouses.

PART VI

◆

RESOLUTION

Why families get surprised, what the recurring patterns are, and how each can be prevented.

CHAPTER 10

Why People Get Surprised by Estate Taxes

Chapter at a Glance

- The eight recurring patterns that produce most estate-tax surprises.
- Why each pattern has a specific cure available during life.
- Why surprises persist despite being preventable — technical rules, long planning horizons, invisible costs.
- Robert's case — a composite illustrating multiple patterns of failure stacking.
- The single most consistent observation: the structures exist, the cures are available, what is missing is engagement.

Most estate-tax surprises come from a small set of recurring patterns. Each is preventable. Each appears with remarkable consistency in actual practice.

The patterns:

- misunderstanding what counts (the gross-estate inclusion question)

- assuming trusts eliminate tax (when many trust structures preserve tax exposure)
- focusing on exemption numbers (when inclusion matters more)
- ignoring retained control (which produces inclusion under sections 2036–2042)
- delaying decisions (which collapses planning windows under section 2035)
- missing state-level exposure (which catches families well below federal thresholds)
- confusing estate tax with inheritance tax (which produces wrong-direction planning)
- missing the basis-step-up trade-off (which produces income-tax surprises)

Estate taxes rarely appear out of nowhere. They appear when structure and timing align in a specific way, and once you know what to look for, you can usually predict the surprise before it happens.

The Eight Recurring Surprise Patterns — In Detail

Each of the eight patterns deserves a brief treatment because each has a specific cure that can be implemented during life.

(1) Inclusion of life insurance the family thought was outside the estate. We treated this in Chapter 4. The cure is to hold the policy in an irrevocable life-insurance trust (ILIT) so that no

incidents of ownership reside with the insured. This must be done more than three years before death (the section 2035 lookback).

(2) Inclusion of property gifted with retained life interests. The classic example is the parent who deeded the family home to children but continued to live there without paying rent. Section 2036 includes the home at full date-of-death value. The cure is either to make the transfer real (parent vacates or pays fair-market rent) or to use a structure designed to avoid section 2036 (QPRT, where appropriate).

(3) Reliance on a trust that doesn't actually exclude. Many families assume that putting assets in a trust removes them from the gross estate. For revocable living trusts, this is wrong — the trust assets are fully includible because the grantor retained the power to amend or revoke. Only properly structured irrevocable trusts remove assets from the gross estate, and the structure has to satisfy the inclusion-rule requirements.

(4) Focus on the exemption to the exclusion of inclusion. Families look at the $13+ million federal exemption, conclude they are well below it, and stop thinking about estate tax. Then state-level exposure surprises them, or the gross estate turns out to include items they had not counted, and the actual tax is real. The cure is to compute the gross estate (per Chapter 4 rules) before assuming the exemption resolves the question.

(5) State-level exposure missed entirely. Twelve states and DC maintain estate taxes; six maintain inheritance taxes. Many state thresholds are sharply lower than the federal. Families that move late in life or that fail to consider state-level exposure routinely face state-tax liability they did not anticipate. The cure is to know the state of domicile and the relevant state thresholds, and to plan accordingly.

(6) Late implementation of structures that have lookback rules. Section 2035's three-year rule, the IRA ten-year-distribution rule, the GST exemption allocation rules, and various state-level lookback rules all penalize late implementation. The cure is to start early — implementing structures five or more years before any plausible death event ensures most of the timing rules are satisfied.

(7) Joint titling that unwinds the basis-step-up. We discussed this in Chapter 8. The cure is to use trust ownership or transfer-on-death deeds rather than joint titling with adult children, particularly for appreciated property.

(8) Lifetime gifts of appreciated property. A common amateur planning move that, for most families, destroys more value through lost basis-step-up than it saves in estate tax. The cure is the rule: do not gift highly appreciated property during life unless the estate-tax savings will exceed the income-tax cost — a calculation that requires specific facts and a specialist's analysis.

Why Surprises Happen Anyway

Three structural reasons explain why these surprises persist despite being preventable.

First, the rules are technical. Sections 2036, 2041, and 2042 are not intuitive. The unified credit, the alternate valuation election, the GST exemption allocation — these are specialist topics that families do not encounter elsewhere in their lives. Specialist advice is needed; specialist advice is sometimes deferred until too late.

Second, the planning horizon is long. Most of the preventive moves require years of advance planning. Families that engage with estate planning only in the last few years of life have far fewer options than families that engage decades earlier. The structures that work best are the ones that have been in place for five, ten, twenty years.

Third, the cost of mistakes is high but invisible during the deceased's lifetime. The family does not see the cost. The deceased does not see the cost. Only the post-death tax filing reveals what the planning failures actually produced. By that point, the cure is no longer available.

> **KEY POINT**
>
> Estate-tax surprises are almost always the result of structures that did not get implemented, not of rules that did not exist. The eight recurring patterns above account for the great majority of real-world surprises. Each has a specific preventive move that, taken during life, would have eliminated the surprise.

What This Looks Like in Practice

A composite of the recurring pattern. Robert was a successful business owner who died at age seventy-eight with a gross estate that ultimately exceeded $20 million. Robert's estate-tax planning had the following characteristics:

- He had heard the federal exemption was high and assumed he was unlikely to face federal tax. (He was right; he was not above the federal exemption when only his probate assets were counted, but his gross estate was sharply higher.)
- He owned $4 million of life insurance individually, never moved into an ILIT, fully includible at death.
- He had transferred his vacation home to his children eight years before death but continued to use it without paying rent. Section 2036 inclusion: $1.5 million.
- He had a revocable living trust holding most of his investment assets. Trust assets fully includible.
- His business interests had appreciated dramatically. He could have implemented a sophisticated structure (GRAT, IDGT) to remove future appreciation from the estate. He did not.
- He lived in a state with an estate tax. He had heard of this but did not view his exposure as material.

When Robert died, his federal estate tax was approximately $3 million (gross estate above the exemption). His state estate tax added another $1.4 million. Combined transfer-tax cost: $4.4

million. The estate's total transfer-tax rate was just over 22% of gross estate.

Each of Robert's planning failures had a specific cure. Each cure had been available to him for years. None had been implemented. The result was a $4.4 million tax bill on what would otherwise have been one of the most favorable transfer-tax positions a family of this wealth could occupy.

Robert's case is unusual only in concentration — most families have one or two of the failures, not all of them. The pattern, however, is the same. The structures exist. The rules are knowable. The cures are available. What is missing is engagement during the years when engagement matters.

What This Looks Like in Practice

A composite of the recurring pattern. Robert was a successful business owner who died at age seventy-eight with a gross estate that ultimately exceeded $20 million. Robert's estate-tax planning had the following characteristics:

- He had heard the federal exemption was high and assumed he was unlikely to face federal tax. (He was right when only his probate assets were counted, but his gross estate was sharply higher.)
- He owned $4 million of life insurance individually, never moved into an ILIT, fully includible at death.

- He had transferred his vacation home to his children eight years before death but continued to use it without paying rent. Section 2036 inclusion: $1.5 million.
- He had a revocable living trust holding most of his investment assets. Trust assets fully includible.
- His business interests had appreciated dramatically. He could have implemented a sophisticated structure to remove future appreciation from the estate. He did not.
- He lived in a state with an estate tax. He had heard of this but did not view his exposure as material.

When Robert died, his federal estate tax was approximately $3 million. His state estate tax added another $1.4 million. Combined transfer-tax cost: $4.4 million. The estate's total transfer-tax rate was just over 22% of gross estate.

Each of Robert's planning failures had a specific cure. Each cure had been available to him for years. None had been implemented. The result was a $4.4 million tax bill on what would otherwise have been one of the most favorable transfer-tax positions a family of this wealth could occupy.

Robert's case is unusual only in concentration — most families have one or two of the failures, not all of them. The pattern, however, is the same. The structures exist. The rules are knowable. The cures are available. What is missing is engagement during the years when engagement matters.

Where We Go From Here

Notes on Practice

The eight recurring patterns of surprise are stable across decades of practice. Counsel who have seen many post-mortem estate-tax filings can usually predict, within fifteen minutes of meeting a new family, which one or two of the eight patterns the family is most exposed to. The intake question — "Walk me through your assets, your structures, and your timeline" — usually surfaces the relevant patterns without specific prompting.

A second observation: the cure for each pattern is specific and well-developed. The structures exist. The rules are knowable. Implementation requires engagement during the years when engagement matters — typically 5-15 years before death. Late engagement is rarely as effective as early engagement, but is always better than none.

Practitioner Patterns — Avoiding the Eight

We have identified the eight recurring surprise patterns. The corresponding planning moves — each implemented during life — are straightforward enough to enumerate.

1. **Hold life insurance in an ILIT.** More than three years before death. Eliminates §2042 inclusion.
2. **Make transfers complete.** If a property is gifted, the donor must actually relinquish all beneficial use, OR pay

fair-market rent. Eliminates §2036 inclusion.

3. **Use limited (not general) powers in trusts.** Drafting precision in trust agreements. Eliminates §2041 inclusion.

4. **Compute the gross estate, not just the probate estate.** Once a year, with counsel. Identifies exposure before it becomes a tax bill.

5. **Verify state-level exposure.** Know the domicile state's threshold and rules. Plan accordingly.

6. **Implement structures early.** Five-plus years before any plausible death event. Avoids §2035 lookback issues.

7. **Use trusts or TOD deeds, not joint titling, with adult children.** Preserves basis-step-up; avoids creditor and control issues.

8. **Don't gift highly appreciated property during life.** Unless the estate-tax savings clearly exceeds the income-tax cost. Specialist analysis required.

When the Patterns Have Already Hit

We have framed the eight patterns as preventable, but families occasionally arrive at counsel after the death has occurred. What can be done at that point?

First, the alternate valuation election (Chapter 6). For estates with assets that have declined in value in the six months following death, the alternate valuation election can reduce the gross estate. The CPA should specifically compute both date-of-death and alternate-date scenarios before filing.

Second, qualified disclaimers. Under IRC §2518, a beneficiary can disclaim an interest in property within nine months of the deceased's death; the disclaimed property passes as if the beneficiary had predeceased. Disclaimer can redirect property to other beneficiaries (often to a credit-shelter trust) in ways that produce a more favorable tax outcome. The technique is fact-specific but powerful in appropriate cases.

Third, late portability relief. As discussed in Chapter 5, estates that missed the timely portability election may obtain relief through Revenue Procedure 2017-34 or §9100 relief in appropriate cases. The relief is not automatic, but the IRS has been relatively lenient in recent years for estates that timely intended to elect.

Fourth, payment-of-tax planning. For estates with material tax owed but limited liquid assets, sections 6166 and 303 provide installment payment and stock-redemption relief, respectively. Section 6161 provides extensions of time to pay (up to ten years) for hardship cases. Each provision is technical and requires deliberate election.

Common Questions, Briefly

I think my deceased relative had estate-tax exposure but the family did not file Form 706. What now?

File now. Late-filed Form 706 is permitted; penalties for late filing and late payment may apply but can sometimes be mitigated for reasonable-cause situations. The statute of limitations on assessment runs from filing, so unfiled returns leave the estate's exposure open indefinitely. Specialist counsel should be engaged immediately; the longer the delay, the more difficult the situation becomes.

How long should I keep estate-tax records?

Indefinitely. The Form 706, supporting appraisals, basis documentation, and beneficiary basis statements (Form 8971) should be retained permanently. Beneficiaries may sell inherited assets decades later and need the documentation to support their basis. Heirs of an estate that filed Form 706 should obtain copies and retain them as part of their permanent tax records.

There is no further chapter. The Conclusion follows.

Figure 10.1

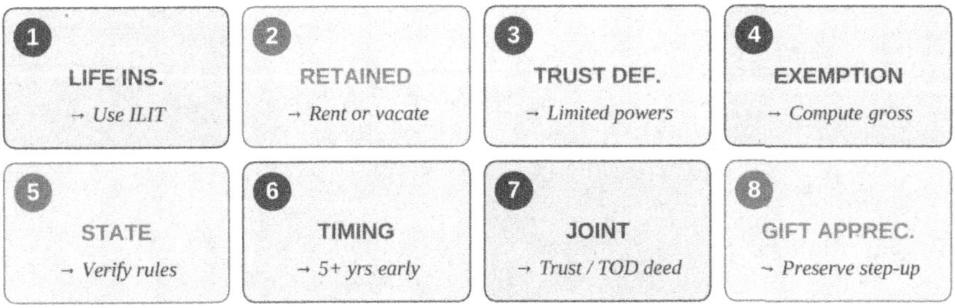

The eight recurring patterns of estate-tax surprise — and the planning cure for each.

KEY POINT

Estate-tax surprises are almost always the result of structures that did not get implemented, not of rules that did not exist. The eight recurring patterns account for most real-world surprises. Each has a specific preventive move available during life.

What This Chapter Has Said

Eight patterns produce most estate-tax surprises: missed inclusion, trust misunderstanding, exemption tunnel vision, retained control, late implementation, missed state exposure, joint titling that loses step-up, and lifetime gifts of appreciated property. Each has a specific cure that must be implemented during life. The structures exist. The rules are knowable. What is missing in surprised estates is engagement during the years when engagement matters. Estate planning is not paperwork and not a confession of mortality — it is the form love takes when it has to outlast the person who felt it.

CONCLUSION

What the System Is For

◆

Estate taxes are not universal, but they are predictable.

They do not apply to everyone.

They do not apply automatically.

They do not apply without reason.

Understanding how estate taxes work — and when they apply — removes fear and replaces it with clarity.

We have spent this volume on the architecture of the American transfer-tax system: what estate taxes are and what they are not, the structural distinction between estate tax and inheritance tax, why the system exists, what gets counted in the gross estate, how the exemption actually works, why timing matters more than amounts, how the gift-tax system links to the estate-tax system, what the basis-step-up is and why it matters more than the estate tax for most families, when capital-gains tax applies and does not, and the recurring patterns of surprise that account for most real-world tax exposure.

What unifies all of this is a single observation: the transfer-tax system is a coordinated regulatory framework, not a single tax. It is designed to address specific structural concerns about wealth concentration and time-shifting. It exempts most families entirely. It applies to those it does apply to in ways that are knowable in advance. And it interacts with the income-tax basis rules in ways that, for most families, matter more than the transfer taxes themselves.

This book does not eliminate estate taxes. It eliminates confusion.

If you understand the system — what it counts, when it applies, how it interacts with the income-tax system — you can plan around it effectively. You can know, in advance, whether your particular family will face exposure. You can implement the structures that minimize the exposure where it exists. You can understand the basis trade-off well enough to avoid the most common amateur planning errors. And you can have, with the people who matter to you, the conversations that turn the tax from an unknown threat into a tractable planning problem.

These are not the conversations the IRS publishes guidance about. They are the conversations the family has to have for itself. The tax law sets the rules; only the family decides how to use them.

"Estate taxes are predictable. They do not apply to everyone. They apply when specific conditions are met. Once those conditions are understood, the fear drops away and the

surprises largely disappear. The system is a framework, not a threat."

And so the book ends where it began — with the same sentence that has anchored each of the four volumes of The Complete Estate & Property Planning Series, and that we hope you will carry with you, and pass forward, long after you have closed these pages:

"Estate planning is not paperwork. It is the form love takes when it has to outlast the person who felt it."

Take the system seriously. Compute your gross estate honestly. Know your state-level exposure. Implement the structures that move appreciable assets out of the estate well before they are needed. Preserve the basis-step-up for everything else. Update your plan when life changes. Tell your CPA and counsel where the originals live.

That work, done in the quiet years before the work is needed, is the highest-leverage protection any family can offer the people who will eventually inherit what it has built. Everything else in this book — the chapters on inclusion, exemption, timing, gift tax, basis-step-up, capital gains, and recurring surprise patterns — is in service of that single act of preparation.

Take care of yours.

— AVOY Publishing

Spring 2026

READER FAQ

Common Questions, Clear Answers

This section addresses, in brief Q-and-A form, the questions readers most commonly ask after finishing the book. The answers are intentionally short. Each one points back to the chapter or chapters where the underlying material is treated in full.

The questions are grouped into three categories: Federal Estate & Gift Tax, State Tax Regimes, and Basis & Capital Gains.

FEDERAL ESTATE & GIFT TAX

Q · WHAT IS THE FEDERAL ESTATE TAX EXEMPTION RIGHT NOW?

A · The applicable exclusion amount changes over time and is indexed for inflation. At the time of writing it is in the low- to mid-eight figures per individual; double that for married couples through portability. The exemption is scheduled for legislative change in the near future. The current figure is a quick search away on the IRS website. See Chapter 5.

Q · WILL MY FAMILY OWE FEDERAL ESTATE TAX?

A · Probably not. Roughly 0.1 to 0.2 percent of American deaths produce a federal estate-tax filing, and even fewer produce actual tax. The exposure is concentrated in estates well into the eight figures and above. Compute your gross estate (per Chapter 4 rules) before assuming, however; surprises live in the inclusion question.

Q · WHO PAYS THE FEDERAL ESTATE TAX?

A · The estate pays. The executor or personal representative files Form 706 and remits any tax due from estate assets before any distribution to beneficiaries. Beneficiaries do not personally owe federal estate tax. See Chapter 1.

Q · WHAT IS PORTABILITY?

A · Portability is the rule (IRC §2010(c)(4)) that allows a surviving spouse to use the deceased spouse's unused federal exemption (the DSUE — deceased spousal unused exclusion). It effectively doubles the available federal exemption for married couples. Portability must be elected on a timely-filed Form 706 from the first spouse to die — even if no estate tax is owed. Missing the election can be expensive. See Chapter 5.

Q · WHAT IS THE GIFT-TAX ANNUAL EXCLUSION?

A · Each donor may give up to the annual exclusion (currently around $19,000, indexed) per donee per year without using any lifetime exemption. Married couples can split gifts, doubling the per-donee amount. Annual-exclusion gifts to as many donees as desired are entirely outside the transfer-tax system. See Chapter 7.

Q · DO I NEED TO FILE A GIFT-TAX RETURN?

A · Yes for most non-annual-exclusion gifts, even when no tax is owed. Form 709 reports the gift, the value, and the use of lifetime exemption. Filing starts the statute of limitations on the IRS's ability to challenge the value. See Chapter 7.

Q · WHAT IS THE GENERATION-SKIPPING TRANSFER TAX?

A · A separate federal tax (IRC Chapter 13) that applies in addition to estate or gift tax on transfers that skip a generation — typically transfers to grandchildren when the parent (the deceased's child) is still alive. The GST exemption is a separate pool from the estate/gift exemption (set at the same dollar level). Mishandled GST tax can produce 40% additional tax on transfers families did not realize were exposed. See Chapter 7.

Q · WHAT IS A QTIP TRUST?

A · A qualified terminable interest property trust — a marital trust structure that gives the surviving spouse income for life while preserving the principal for remainder beneficiaries (typically the deceased's children from a prior marriage). The QTIP qualifies for the marital deduction at the first death and is includible in the surviving spouse's estate at the second death. See Glossary and Chapter 5.

Q · WHAT IS THE UNLIMITED MARITAL DEDUCTION?

A · The rule (IRC §2056) that allows unlimited transfers to a US citizen surviving spouse without federal estate tax. Combined with the unlimited gift-tax marital deduction (§2523), spouses can move any amount between themselves without federal transfer tax. The deduction does not eliminate eventual tax; it defers it to the second spouse's death. See Chapter 5.

Q · WHAT IS AN ILIT?

A · An irrevocable life-insurance trust. A structure designed to hold life-insurance policies on the grantor's life so that the proceeds are not includible in the grantor's gross estate at death. The trust must be irrevocable, the grantor cannot hold incidents of ownership, and the structure must be in place more than three years before death (the §2035 lookback) to be fully effective. See Chapter 4.

STATE TAX REGIMES

Q · DOES MY STATE HAVE AN ESTATE TAX?

A · Twelve states plus DC currently impose an estate tax. The estate-tax states (representative): Connecticut, DC, Hawaii, Illinois, Maine, Maryland, Massachusetts, Minnesota, New York, Oregon, Rhode Island, Vermont, Washington. Thresholds are typically much lower than the federal exemption — Oregon is $1 million, Massachusetts is $2 million. Verify current law. See Chapter 2 and Table 2.3.

Q · DOES MY STATE HAVE AN INHERITANCE TAX?

A · Six states do: Iowa, Kentucky, Maryland, Nebraska, New Jersey, Pennsylvania. Inheritance tax is paid by the beneficiary, not the estate, and rates typically rise with the distance of the relationship. Spouses are exempt in every inheritance-tax state. See Chapter 2 and Table 2.2.

Q · CAN I AVOID STATE ESTATE TAX BY MOVING TO A DIFFERENT STATE?

A · Sometimes. State estate tax applies to the estate of a person domiciled in that state at death. Genuine domicile change before death (with all the indicia — driver's license, voter registration, primary residence, time spent) eliminates exposure. But out-of-state real property may remain subject to ancillary state-level tax. The move must be real, not cosmetic. See Chapter 2.

Q · DOES PORTABILITY APPLY AT THE STATE LEVEL?

A · It depends on the state. Some states recognize federal portability for state purposes; others do not. Where it does not apply, married couples must use credit-shelter (bypass) trusts to preserve both spouses' state exemptions. See Chapter 5.

BASIS & CAPITAL GAINS

Q · WHAT IS BASIS-STEP-UP?

A · The rule (IRC §1014) that resets the income-tax basis of inherited property to the fair market value at the date of the deceased's death. Pre-death appreciation becomes invisible to the income-tax system. For most American families, this rule matters more financially than the estate tax itself. See Chapter 8.

Q · DO I OWE CAPITAL-GAINS TAX WHEN I INHERIT PROPERTY?

A · No. Inheritance is not a sale event. Capital-gains tax applies only when you eventually sell. With the basis-step-up, the gain on a prompt sale is usually zero or small. See Chapter 9.

Q · WHAT HAPPENS IF I GIFT APPRECIATED PROPERTY DURING LIFE?

A · The donee takes your original basis (the carryover basis rule, §1015), not a stepped-up basis. The donee will owe capital-gains tax on the full appreciation when they eventually sell. For most families, this is exactly backward — gifting appreciated property loses the basis-step-up the family would otherwise get at death. See Chapter 8.

Q · DO RETIREMENT ACCOUNTS GET A BASIS-STEP-UP?

A · No. IRAs, 401(k)s, and similar tax-deferred accounts do not receive a basis-step-up. The beneficiary inherits the pre-tax balance and pays ordinary income tax on distributions. This is one of the more important asymmetries in inheritance tax planning. See Chapter 8.

Q · DOES THE BASIS-STEP-UP APPLY TO PROPERTY HELD JOINTLY?

A · Partially. Joint property with a non-spouse receives only a half step-up (the deceased's half steps up; the survivor's half retains its original basis). Joint property held by spouses in a community-property state, or as community property with right of survivorship, receives a full double step-up. Joint property held by spouses in a non-community-property state receives a half step-up. See Chapter 8 and Table 8.1.

Q · WHAT IS THE SECTION 121 HOME-SALE EXCLUSION?

A · The rule (IRC §121) that allows up to $250,000 ($500,000 for married couples filing jointly) of capital gain on the sale of a primary residence to be excluded from income. The seller must have owned and used the property as a primary residence for at least two of the five years preceding sale. For inheritors who later occupy and sell, this stacks with the basis-step-up. See Chapter 9.

Q · I INHERITED A HOUSE. WHEN SHOULD I SELL IT?

A · If you intend to sell, sooner is generally better. The basis-step-up captures the date-of-death value; further appreciation after inheritance is taxable. Selling within the first year usually produces little or no capital-gains tax. Holding for years and then selling means you owe tax on the post-death appreciation. See Chapter 9.

GLOSSARY OF TAX TERMS

◆

This glossary covers the principal terms used in this book, in alphabetical order. Each entry includes a brief definition and, where helpful, a cross-reference to the chapter where the term is treated in fuller context.

Adjusted Taxable Gifts

Lifetime taxable gifts (other than annual-exclusion and marital/charitable) added back to the estate-tax computation to compute the federal estate tax under the unified credit system. See Chapter 7.

Alternate Valuation Date

An election under IRC §2032 to value the gross estate as of the date six months after death, rather than the date of death, when doing so produces lower estate tax. Election made on the first-filed Form 706. See Chapter 6.

Annual Exclusion (Gift Tax)

The amount each donor may give to each donee each year without using lifetime exemption (currently around $19,000, indexed). See Chapter 7.

Applicable Exclusion Amount

The federal estate-tax exemption — the amount of taxable estate that can pass without federal estate tax. Indexed annually. See Chapter 5.

Basis

The tax-significant cost of an asset, used to determine capital gain or loss on eventual sale. See Chapter 8.

Basis Step-Up (IRC §1014)

The rule resetting inherited property's basis to fair market value at date of death. Eliminates pre-death appreciation from the income-tax base. See Chapter 8.

Bypass Trust (Credit-Shelter Trust)

A trust funded at the first spouse's death with the deceased spouse's exemption equivalent, bypassing the surviving spouse's estate. Used to preserve both spouses' exemptions in states without state-level portability. See Chapter 5.

Carryover Basis (IRC §1015)

The basis rule for property received as a gift — donee takes donor's original basis. Distinguished from stepped-up basis for inherited property. See Chapter 8.

Charitable Deduction

Unlimited deduction from the gross estate for transfers to qualified charities (IRC §2055). Parallels the gift-tax charitable deduction. See Chapter 5.

Cliff (Estate-Tax Cliff)

A state estate-tax structure under which the entire estate (not just the amount above threshold) becomes subject to tax when the threshold is crossed. Used historically by Massachusetts and (in modified form) New York. See Chapter 5.

Community Property

Property acquired by either spouse during marriage in one of nine community-property states; presumed to be owned equally by both. Receives particularly favorable basis treatment (double step-up under §1014(b)(6)) at first death. See Chapter 8.

Date of Death Valuation

The default valuation rule — assets in the gross estate valued at fair market value as of the date of the deceased's death. See Chapter 6.

Deceased Spousal Unused Exclusion (DSUE)

The amount of federal exemption unused by the first spouse to die; available to the surviving spouse if portability is elected on the first spouse's Form 706. See Chapter 5.

Estate Tax

A tax on the transfer of wealth at death, imposed on the estate (not the beneficiaries). Federal version (IRC Chapter 11) and state-level versions exist. See Chapter 1.

Form 706

United States Estate (and Generation-Skipping Transfer) Tax Return. Filed by the executor for estates exceeding the filing threshold or to elect portability. See Chapter 5.

Form 709

United States Gift (and Generation-Skipping Transfer) Tax Return. Filed by the donor for taxable gifts and to allocate GST exemption. See Chapter 7.

Generation-Skipping Transfer Tax (GST)

A separate federal tax (IRC Chapter 13) on transfers that skip a generation. Has its own exemption pool, set at the same dollar level as the estate/gift exemption. See Chapter 7.

Gift Tax

Federal tax on transfers of property by gift during life (IRC Chapter 12). Paid by the donor. Coordinated with estate tax through the unified credit. See Chapter 7.

Grantor Trust

A trust whose income is taxed to the grantor for federal income-tax purposes. Common feature of estate-tax planning structures (intentionally defective grantor trusts). See Chapters 6 and 8.

Gross Estate

The total value of all property included in the deceased's estate for federal estate-tax purposes — broader than the probate estate. Includes life insurance owned by the deceased, retirement accounts, jointly held property, certain transferred assets, and more. See Chapter 4.

ILIT (Irrevocable Life Insurance Trust)

A trust holding life-insurance policies, structured so that proceeds are not includible in the insured's gross estate. See Chapter 4.

Incidents of Ownership

Powers over a life-insurance policy that, if held by the insured, cause the proceeds to be included in the insured's gross estate (IRC §2042). Includes the right to change beneficiary, surrender, assign, or borrow against the policy. See Chapter 4.

Income in Respect of a Decedent (IRD)

Income earned by the deceased before death but received after death — does NOT receive a basis step-up; taxed as ordinary income to the recipient. Common with retirement accounts and accrued but unpaid compensation. See Chapter 8.

Inheritance Tax

A state-level tax on beneficiaries who receive property from a deceased person. Six states impose one. Rates typically vary with the relationship. See Chapter 2.

Lifetime Exemption (Lifetime Credit)

The amount of lifetime gifts a donor may make without producing actual gift tax owed (above the annual exclusion). Coordinated with the estate-tax exemption through the unified credit. See Chapter 7.

Marital Deduction

Unlimited deduction from the gross estate for transfers to a US citizen surviving spouse (IRC §2056). Parallels the gift-tax marital deduction. See Chapter 5.

Net Investment Income Tax (NIIT)

A 3.8% federal tax (IRC §1411) on net investment income for high-income taxpayers. Applies on top of long-term capital-gains rates. See Chapter 9.

Portability

The rule allowing a surviving spouse to use the deceased spouse's unused federal exemption. Election required on first spouse's Form 706. See Chapter 5.

Power of Appointment

The right to direct trust property to particular beneficiaries. A general power (exercisable in favor of self, estate, or creditors) causes inclusion in the holder's gross estate (IRC §2041). Limited powers do not. See Chapter 4.

Probate Estate

The set of assets that pass through probate at death. Distinguished from the gross estate, which is broader. See Chapter 4.

QPRT (Qualified Personal Residence Trust)

A trust to which the grantor transfers a residence while retaining the right to occupy for a term of years, structured to remove the residence from the gross estate at a discounted gift-tax cost. See Chapter 6.

QTIP (Qualified Terminable Interest Property)

A marital trust giving the surviving spouse income for life while preserving principal for remainder beneficiaries. Qualifies for the marital deduction at first death; includible in surviving spouse's estate at second death. See Chapter 5.

Section 2032A (Special Use Valuation)

An election to value qualified farm or closely held business real property based on its actual use rather than its highest-and-best use. Capped reduction. See Chapter 6.

Section 2035 (Three-Year Rule)

The rule pulling certain transfers made within three years of death back into the gross estate — most importantly, life-insurance transfers and gift tax paid. See Chapter 4.

Section 2036 (Retained Interest Rule)

The rule including in the gross estate property the deceased transferred during life but in which the deceased retained a substantial interest or power. Classic example: a parent deeds the home to children but continues to live there. See Chapter 4.

Section 2041 (Powers of Appointment)

Includes in the gross estate property over which the deceased held a general power of appointment at death. See Chapter 4.

Section 2042 (Life Insurance)

Includes in the gross estate life-insurance proceeds payable on the deceased's life if the deceased held incidents of ownership at death. See Chapter 4.

Section 121 Exclusion

Income-tax exclusion of up to $250k single / $500k joint of capital gain on sale of primary residence. Requires 2-of-5-year ownership and use. See Chapter 9.

Section 1014 (Basis Step-Up)

The rule resetting inherited property's basis to fair market value at date of death. See Chapter 8.

Section 1015 (Carryover Basis)

The rule applying carryover basis to property received as a gift. See Chapter 8.

Step Transaction Doctrine

A judicial doctrine collapsing a series of formally separate transactions into a single transaction for tax purposes when they are integrated parts of a single plan. Affects estate-tax planning when transfers are too closely sequenced.

Sunset Provision

A statutory provision causing a tax rule to expire on a specified date unless extended. The current high federal exemption is subject to a sunset that, absent further legislation, will reduce the exemption substantially. See Chapter 5.

Tentative Tax

The federal estate tax computed before subtraction of the unified credit. Computed on the sum of taxable estate plus adjusted taxable gifts at the rate schedule. See Chapter 5.

Unified Credit

The credit against tentative tax equal to the credit equivalent of the applicable exclusion amount. Covers both lifetime gifts and at-death transfers in a single pool. See Chapter 7.

Unlimited Marital Deduction

See Marital Deduction. Allows unlimited transfers to a US citizen surviving spouse without federal transfer tax.

Valuation Discount

Reduction in reported value of certain transferred assets (typically minority interests in closely held businesses, fractional interests in real property) reflecting lack of marketability or lack of control. Subject to IRS challenge.

BIBLIOGRAPHY & REFERENCE GUIDE

◆

This bibliography lists the principal sources consulted in preparing this volume, organized by category. It is not exhaustive. It is intended as a reading map for the serious reader who wishes to investigate the underlying material in greater depth.

STATUTORY AND REGULATORY SOURCES

Internal Revenue Code, Subtitle B (Estate and Gift Taxes): Chapter 11 (Estate Tax), Chapter 12 (Gift Tax), Chapter 13 (Tax on Generation-Skipping Transfers), and Chapter 14 (Special Valuation Rules).

Internal Revenue Code, Subchapter J (Estates, Trusts, Beneficiaries, and Decedents).

Internal Revenue Code §1014 (basis of property acquired from a decedent), §1015 (basis of property acquired by gift), §121 (exclusion of gain on principal residence), §1411 (Net Investment Income Tax).

Treasury Regulations under each of the above Code sections — available at the Treasury Department and Code of Federal Regulations websites.

IRS Form 706 (United States Estate (and Generation-Skipping Transfer) Tax Return) and instructions; IRS Form 709 (United States Gift (and Generation-Skipping Transfer) Tax Return) and instructions.

IRS Publication 559 (Survivors, Executors, and Administrators); IRS Publication 950 (Introduction to Estate and Gift Taxes).

TREATISES

Pennell, Federal Wealth Transfer Taxation (West). Standard advanced text on federal estate, gift, and generation-skipping transfer taxes.

Bittker & Lokken, Federal Taxation of Income, Estates and Gifts (Thomson Reuters). Multi-volume treatise covering all transfer-tax topics in extended depth.

Bogert, Bogert & Hess, The Law of Trusts and Trustees (3d ed., Thomson Reuters). Standard American treatise on trust law, including transfer-tax interactions.

Restatement (Third) of Property: Wills and Other Donative Transfers, American Law Institute. Synthesis of American law on intestate succession, will substitutes, and post-mortem transfer.

PRACTITIONER GUIDES

American College of Trust and Estate Counsel (ACTEC) Commentaries — practitioner guidance on the ethics and technical practice of transfer-tax representation.

Sitkoff & Dukeminier, Wills, Trusts, and Estates (Aspen Casebook Series, Wolters Kluwer). The leading academic casebook in the field.

Stephens, Maxfield, Lind, Calfee & Smith, Federal Estate and Gift Taxation (Thomson Reuters). Standard practitioner treatise.

Trust Made Simple (AVOY Publishing, 2026; Book 1 of The Complete Estate & Property Planning Series), Probate Explained (Book 2), and Property After Death (Book 3) — the companion volumes treating the trust, the probate process, and post-mortem real-property disposition in the same plain-language style.

PERIODICALS

Estate Planning journal (Thomson Reuters), monthly. Practitioner-oriented coverage of transfer-tax developments.

Trusts & Estates magazine, monthly. Long-running industry publication.

Tax Notes Federal (Tax Analysts), weekly. Detailed coverage of federal tax developments, including frequent transfer-tax content.

ACTEC Law Journal (American College of Trust and Estate Counsel), three times annually. Scholarly.

ONLINE AND PRACTITIONER RESOURCES

IRS website (irs.gov) — primary source for current exemption amounts, forms, and guidance.

ACTEC website (actec.org) — leading professional society for trust and estate practitioners.

American Bar Association, Section of Real Property, Trust and Estate Law (americanbar.org/groups/real_property_trust_estate).

Tax Policy Center (taxpolicycenter.org). Independent analysis of federal and state transfer-tax issues.

State Department of Revenue / Taxation websites — authoritative for current state exemption amounts and rates.

ABOUT THE PUBLISHER

◆

AVOY, LLC ("AVOY Publishing") is the publishing imprint of AVOY, LLC, a privately held company headquartered in the United States. AVOY Publishing exists to bring institutional-grade reference material on private wealth, legacy planning, family governance, and the procedural realities of American private law to readers who would otherwise rely on marketing brochures and law-review articles.

The Complete Estate & Property Planning Series is the imprint's flagship project — a four-book institutional reference that, taken together, addresses the four pillars of American post-mortem asset transfer: the trust as instrument, the probate process, the disposition of real property, and the transfer-tax regime. Each volume in the series is built to the same standard: a sophisticated subject treated with care, written for the intelligent reader rather than the specialist, structured for both first reading and long-term reference, and produced to a physical and editorial quality that respects the seriousness of the subject.

The four books in The Complete Estate & Property Planning Series:

- Book 1 — Trust Made Simple

- Book 2 — Probate Explained
- Book 3 — Property After Death
- Book 4 — Estate Taxes Explained (this volume)

Estate Taxes Explained is Book 4 of the series, completing the four-volume reference. Where Trust Made Simple establishes the principal probate-avoidance vehicle, Probate Explained treats the alternative court-supervised transfer, and Property After Death drills into real-property disposition, this volume treats the tax overlay that shapes the entire structure for substantial estates — and that, even for estates well below the federal threshold, frequently shapes outcomes through state-level regimes, gift-tax interactions, and the fundamental income-tax basis-step-up rules.

AVOY Publishing books are distributed in print (paperback and hardcover), Kindle eBook, and audiobook formats through Amazon and other retailers.

Inquiries: ap@avoyhq.com

ABOUT THE AUTHOR

◆

A. Perkins writes for people who would rather understand a thing than be told what to think about it.

A #1 Amazon bestselling author, former United States Air Force nuclear missile launch officer, holder of an MBA, and a working chief executive, he has spent his career at the intersection of high-stakes systems and ordinary human consequence. Born in Mississippi and raised in East St. Louis, Illinois, he is among the rare voices in legacy-planning literature to have navigated generational poverty, institutional pressure, and significant personal and financial trials — and to have emerged with a single, durable conviction: that everyday Americans, properly informed and properly equipped, can build extraordinary protection for the people they love.

His prior body of work — including the bestselling 21 Bars: Poetry from the Inside and Urban Poetry & Truth: The Echo of the Streets; Whispers to Mom: A Collection of Poems Celebrating Love, Resilience, and Mothers; The Intimacy Life Cycle: Fire – Fizzle – Fire; Stillness Starts Here; Beyond the Vail: An Awakening; Whispers of Love and Life — Part II; the institutional-grade reference volumes Trust Made Simple (Book 1), Probate Explained (Book 2), and Property After Death

(Book 3) of The Complete Estate & Property Planning Series — spans poetry, mindfulness, and the lived terrain of resilience, alongside the legacy-planning subjects he has been studying for more than a decade. Across twenty-nine prior volumes — each released in both print and audiobook — and three Amazon bestseller categories, he has built a readership that returns to him for one reason above all: the willingness to tell the truth in plain language.

Estate Taxes Explained is his thirtieth book in print, the fourth dedicated to the field of legacy planning, and Book 4 of The Complete Estate & Property Planning Series — completing the four-volume reference that began with Trust Made Simple (Book 1), continued through Probate Explained (Book 2) and Property After Death (Book 3), and concludes with this volume. It grows out of more than a decade of practical, personal experience with the administration of estates and trusts, years of close study of the federal and state transfer-tax regimes, and the conviction that the transfer-tax system — properly understood — is far more predictable than the fear surrounding it would suggest. Like every prior title in his catalog, it is also available in an audiobook edition.

Mr. Perkins is the founder and chief executive of AVOY, LLC, parent of AVOY Publishing and The Complete Estate & Property Planning Series. He continues to write, teach, and speak on protection, legacy, and the long arithmetic of family wealth.

For editorial and speaking inquiries: ap@avoyhq.com

PART

◆

APPENDICES

Reference material — checklists, samples, and supplementary tools.

APPENDIX A

Tax at a Glance

This appendix is a single-card reference summarizing the American transfer-tax landscape in one place. Verify current figures with the IRS or current state guidance.

Table A.1

Element	Description	Applies
Federal estate tax	Tax on transfers of wealth at death; paid by estate	Estates exceeding applicable exclusion amount
Federal gift tax	Tax on transfers of wealth during life; paid by donor	Gifts using lifetime exemption
Federal GST tax	Tax on transfers skipping a generation	Transfers exceeding GST exemption
Annual exclusion	Per-donee gift tax exclusion (~$19k indexed)	Each donor / each donee / each year
Marital deduction	Unlimited deduction for transfers to US citizen spouse	Estate and gift tax (parallel rules)
Charitable deduction	Unlimited deduction for transfers to qualified charity	Estate and gift tax (parallel rules)
Portability (DSUE)	Surviving spouse uses deceased spouse's unused federal exemption	Election on first spouse's Form 706
Basis step-up (§1014)	Inherited property basis = FMV at date of death	Most assets except IRAs and IRD

Federal transfer-tax system at a glance.

APPENDIX B

State Estate & Inheritance Tax Map

Tables 2.2 and 2.3 in Chapter 2 set out the principal state-by-state thresholds. This appendix provides a consolidated view.

Twelve states plus DC currently impose an estate tax. Six states impose an inheritance tax. Two states impose both. Approximately thirty-two states impose neither.

Estate-Tax States (12 + DC)

Connecticut, District of Columbia, Hawaii, Illinois, Maine, Maryland, Massachusetts, Minnesota, New York, Oregon, Rhode Island, Vermont, Washington.

Inheritance-Tax States (6)

Iowa, Kentucky, Maryland, Nebraska, New Jersey, Pennsylvania.

Both Taxes (Maryland)

Maryland is currently the only state with both an estate tax and an inheritance tax. New Jersey previously had both but has phased out its estate tax.

Neither Tax (~32 states)

Most southern, western, and midwestern states impose no transfer tax of either kind. Verify current law for any state of interest.

APPENDIX C

The Form 706 Filing Checklist

The Form 706 (federal estate-tax return) is required for estates exceeding the filing threshold or for any spouse wishing to elect portability. This checklist covers the principal items the executor and CPA should assemble.

Documents to Gather

- Death certificate (multiple originals).
- Will and any codicils; trust agreement and amendments; powers of appointment.
- Last three years of personal income-tax returns.
- Last three years of gift-tax returns (Form 709), if any.
- Real-property deeds for every parcel owned, jointly held, or in trust.
- Statements for all bank, brokerage, retirement accounts as of date of death.
- Life-insurance policies — original or duplicate copies, including beneficiary designations.
- Closely held business documents — operating agreements, valuations, recent financials.

· Fiduciary correspondence — trust statements, partnership K-1s, estate income.

· Appraisals — real property, business interests, art, jewelry, collectibles.

Decisions to Make

· Whether to elect alternate valuation date (§2032).

· Whether to elect special use valuation for qualifying farm/business real estate (§2032A).

· Whether to elect portability (DSUE) — must be made on first-filed Form 706.

· How to allocate GST exemption to particular transfers and trusts.

· Which deductions to claim on Form 706 vs. Form 1041 (estate income return).

· Whether to file protectively if exposure is uncertain.

Filing Mechanics

· Form 706 due nine months after date of death.

· Six-month extension available (Form 4768).

· Tax payment deadline is generally nine months after death (extension does not extend payment).

· Estate-tax closing letter (or transcript via online IRS account) issues several months after acceptance.

· Statute of limitations on assessment is generally three years from filing.

APPENDIX D

Common Tax Forms and What They Mean

Estate-tax practice generates a great deal of paper. This appendix names the forms that recur most often.

Table D.1

Form	Purpose	Filed by
Form 706	Federal estate (and GST) tax return	Executor (or attorney/CPA on executor's behalf)
Form 706-NA	Estate-tax return for nonresident aliens	Executor of nonresident alien estate
Form 709	Federal gift (and GST) tax return	Donor (each year as needed)
Form 1040	Final personal income-tax return for deceased	Executor (covering year of death)
Form 1041	Estate's annual income-tax return	Executor (each year of administration)
Form 1099-R	Distribution from retirement account	Custodian (sent to beneficiary)
Schedule K-1	Beneficiary's share of estate or trust income	Estate or trust
Form 4768	Application for extension of time to file estate-tax return	Executor
Form 8971	Information regarding beneficiaries' basis	Executor (for estates filing 706 after July 2015)
Form W-9 / SS-4	Employer ID for estate / trust	Executor / trustee at start of administration

Common federal tax forms in estate-tax practice.

APPENDIX E

Sample Letter to Heirs Regarding Tax Matters

After a death, beneficiaries often have tax-related questions and need information from the executor and the estate's CPA. A short letter, sent to each beneficiary within the first few months of administration, prevents many of the questions and sets expectations.

The following is a sample, adapted from common practitioner conventions.

SAMPLE

To: All beneficiaries of the [Name] Estate. Date: [Date]. I am writing in my capacity as executor of the estate to share information about how the estate's tax matters will be handled. The estate's CPA is [name, firm]. The estate's attorney is [name, firm]. (1) Estate-level tax filings. The estate will file a federal estate-tax return (Form 706) [if applicable]. The return is due nine months from the date of death; we may extend the filing deadline by six months but the tax-payment deadline cannot be extended. The estate will file an annual income-tax return (Form 1041) for each year of administration on income earned during that year. (2) State filings. The estate will file the [state] estate-tax return. State threshold is [amount]; the estate is/is not above that threshold. (3) What you will receive. You will receive a Schedule K-1 each year reporting your share of any estate income for that year. The K-1 must be reported on your personal income-tax return. You may also receive Form 8971 reporting your basis in any inherited assets — preserve this; it documents your basis-step-up. (4) Capital-gains considerations. Inherited property generally receives a stepped-up basis under IRC §1014. If you sell inherited property soon after distribution, you will likely have little or no capital gain. If you hold and later sell, the gain is measured from the date-of-death value. Retirement accounts (IRAs) do NOT receive basis step-up and produce ordinary income on distribution. (5) Your personal CPA. We strongly suggest you consult your own CPA before any distribution. The estate's CPA represents the estate; you should have your own advisor for personal tax planning. (6) Questions. Direct tax questions to [estate CPA, name and email]; direct administrative questions to me. With regard, [Name], Executor.

APPENDIX F

Annotated Reading List for the Serious Reader

Readers who finish this volume and want to continue should consider the following sources.

Pennell, Federal Wealth Transfer Taxation. The leading advanced treatise. Useful for the reader who wants the tax law in extended discussion.

Sitkoff & Dukeminier, Wills, Trusts, and Estates. The leading academic casebook. Useful for context.

Bittker & Lokken, Federal Taxation of Income, Estates and Gifts. Multi-volume treatise covering the entire transfer-tax landscape in extensive depth.

Trust Made Simple (AVOY Publishing, 2026). Book 1 of The Complete Estate & Property Planning Series. The foundational treatment of trust structures, including the trust-funding discipline that underlies most tax-driven planning structures.

Probate Explained (AVOY Publishing, 2026). Book 2 of the series. Treats the probate process in plain-language depth.

Property After Death (AVOY Publishing, 2026). Book 3 of the series. Real-property disposition at death — the asset Americans most often own and most often misunderstand.

IRS Statistics of Income reports (irs.gov/statistics). Annual data on actual estate-tax filings, exemption use, and rate-of-tax statistics. Useful for understanding actual (versus assumed) impact.

Tax Policy Center reports (taxpolicycenter.org). Independent analysis of federal and state transfer-tax issues.

APPENDIX G

The Twelve-Month Estate-Tax Calendar

This calendar is a month-by-month overview of an estate-tax administration. Actual cases vary.

Table G.1

Month	Principal activities	Tax milestones
1	Engage estate counsel and CPA. Begin asset inventory.	Order EIN for estate (Form SS-4).
2-3	Gather documents. Obtain appraisals.	First Form 1041 may be due if year crosses tax year-end.
4-6	Complete inventory. Begin Form 706 preparation.	Decedent's final Form 1040 due April 15.
7-9	Form 706 finalized; alternate valuation election decided.	Form 706 due nine months after death (extendable).
9-12	Tax payment due. Form 706 filed.	GST allocations completed.
12-15	Estate income returns filed (Form 1041) for first year.	Schedule K-1s issued to beneficiaries.
18-24	IRS review of Form 706; closing letter or transcript.	Statute begins running on filing.

Twelve-month estate-tax administration calendar.

APPENDIX H

The Family Tax Communication Framework

Tax matters during estate administration generate questions from beneficiaries that the executor cannot always answer. A structured communication framework reduces friction and prevents misunderstanding.

Quarterly Update From Executor

Once a quarter, the executor should send a brief written update to all beneficiaries covering:

1. **Where the tax filings stand.** Form 706 status, Form 1041 status, state filings.
2. **What has been paid.** Estate-tax payments, professional fees, ongoing expenses.
3. **What is upcoming.** Filing deadlines, decisions requiring beneficiary input.
4. **What beneficiaries should expect.** K-1s for tax filings, basis statements (Form 8971), preliminary distribution timing.
5. **Anything else they need to know.** Plain language.

What to Tell Beneficiaries About Their Own Returns

Beneficiaries who receive estate income, retirement-account distributions, or in-kind asset distributions need to report these correctly on their personal income-tax returns. The executor should:

- Issue Schedule K-1 promptly each year, as soon as the estate's Form 1041 is finalized.
- Provide Form 8971 (basis statement) to beneficiaries who receive in-kind distributions of assets.
- Recommend that each beneficiary consult their own CPA, separately from the estate's CPA.
- Not provide tax advice to beneficiaries — that is the beneficiary's CPA's role.

APPENDIX I

Subject Index

The following index lists principal terms and concepts treated in this volume, alphabetically, with the chapter where each is treated.

APPENDIX J

A Reader's Quick-Start Guide

If you are facing an immediate estate-tax question, this appendix is a single-page distillation of the most important early steps.

Three Questions to Answer First

1. **Is the deceased's gross estate above the federal exemption?** Compute per Chapter 4 rules. Most estates are not — but verify, don't assume.
2. **What state was the deceased domiciled in?** Twelve states + DC have estate tax with thresholds far below federal. Six states have inheritance tax. Verify.
3. **Is portability worth electing on Form 706?** If the deceased was married, almost always yes. The election preserves the unused exemption for the surviving spouse and protects against future exposure. Even if no tax is owed.

First-Month Actions

- Engage estate counsel and a CPA experienced with estate-tax filings.
- Order EIN for the estate.

- Begin gathering financial documents — bank statements, brokerage statements, life-insurance policies, business documents, real-property deeds.
- Obtain date-of-death appraisals for real property and major assets.
- Note the nine-month Form 706 deadline.

What to Read in This Book First

Chapter 4 (gross-estate inclusion), Chapter 5 (federal exemption and portability), and Chapter 8 (basis-step-up). Those three chapters cover the immediate questions for most estates.

APPENDIX K

Notes on The Complete Estate & Property Planning Series

The Complete Estate & Property Planning Series is AVOY Publishing's flagship project — a four-book institutional reference that treats, taken together, the four pillars of American post-mortem asset transfer.

The Four Books in the Series

1. **Book 1 — Trust Made Simple.** The foundational treatment of the trust as instrument.
2. **Book 2 — Probate Explained.** The institutional-grade explanation of probate itself.
3. **Book 3 — Property After Death.** How real property moves at and after death.
4. **Book 4 — Estate Taxes Explained (this volume).** The capstone — federal and state transfer-tax regime, basis-step-up rules, and the planning architecture.

Reading the Series Together

The four volumes share a deliberate architecture. Trust Made Simple establishes the principal probate-avoidance vehicle. Probate Explained treats the alternative — the court-supervised transfer that occurs when no trust applies. Property After Death drills into the asset category that produces the most family pain regardless of which path applies. Estate Taxes Explained (this volume) treats the tax overlay that shapes the entire structure for substantial estates.

Read in order, the series gives you a complete mental model of post-mortem asset transfer in American private law. Read individually — each volume stands alone — and you will still have a definitive treatment of the subject the title names.

Future Editions and Notification

AVOY Publishing intends to maintain each volume in the series with periodic editions reflecting changes in tax law, state statutes, and practice. Estate Taxes Explained in particular will require updates as the federal exemption is adjusted by legislation. Readers who would like to receive notice of future editions and updates can request to be added to the series notification list at ap@avoyhq.com.

APPENDIX L

Chapter-by-Chapter Summary

This summary captures the principal idea of each chapter.

Chapter 1 — What Estate Taxes Are — and What They Are Not
Estate taxes are taxes on the transfer of wealth at death, imposed on the estate, not on beneficiaries. They are not income taxes, not inheritance taxes, and not automatic. Most American estates pay none.

Chapter 2 — Estate Tax vs. Inheritance Tax
Estate tax is paid by the estate; inheritance tax is paid by the beneficiary. The federal government has no inheritance tax. Twelve states + DC have estate tax; six states have inheritance tax. Two regimes are independent and carry different planning consequences.

Chapter 3 — Why Estate Taxes Exist
Estate taxes exist for structural reasons: regulating wealth concentration, coordinating the lifetime/at-death boundary, preventing time-shifting through retained control. Most estates are designed to be exempt; the system exempts most families entirely.

Chapter 4 — What Gets Counted in an Estate

Estate-tax surprises live in the gross-estate inclusion question. Life insurance, retained interests, powers of appointment, joint property, and pre-death gifts produce most of the surprise inclusions. Sections 2035-2042 govern.

Chapter 5 — The Estate Tax Exemption

The federal exemption applies after inclusion is determined. Portability (DSUE) effectively doubles the exemption for married couples, but requires election. State exemptions are much lower than federal — the real exposure for many families is at the state level.

Chapter 6 — Why Timing Matters More Than Amounts

Estate-tax exposure is fixed at the date of death. Alternate valuation may help in falling markets. Timing of when ownership truly changed produces most of the inclusion surprises. Plan early — section 2035's three-year lookback catches late implementation.

Chapter 7 — Gift Taxes and Their Connection to Estate Taxes

Gift tax and estate tax are coordinated through the unified credit. Annual exclusion, medical/educational exclusion, and marital/charitable deductions allow substantial transfers without using exemption. GST tax is a separate parallel system. Annual-exclusion gifting is the most reliable long-term planning tool.

Chapter 8 — Basis and the Step-Up Explained Simply

The basis-step-up at death (§1014) eliminates pre-death appreciation from the income-tax base. For most families, this rule matters more financially than the estate tax itself. Lifetime gifting of appreciated property loses the step-up and is usually a poor planning move.

Chapter 9 — Capital Gains After Death

Capital-gains tax applies on sale, not on inheritance. Inherited property is automatically long-term-held for rate purposes. Section 121 exclusion applies for inheritors who occupy and sell the residence. Selling soon after inheritance captures the step-up most cleanly.

Chapter 10 — Why People Get Surprised by Estate Taxes

Eight recurring patterns account for most surprises: inclusion missed, trusts misunderstood, exemption focus, retained control, late implementation, state exposure missed, joint titling errors, and lifetime gifts of appreciated property. Each has a specific cure available during life.

APPENDIX M

Generation-Skipping Transfer Reference

The generation-skipping transfer (GST) tax under Internal Revenue Code Chapter 13 is the most technical of the federal transfer taxes and the one most likely to surprise ordinary practitioners. This appendix collects the principal rules in one place.

What the GST Tax Does

The GST tax imposes a flat 40% federal tax on transfers that skip a generation — typically transfers from a grandparent to a grandchild, where the parent (the deceased's child) is still alive at the time of the transfer. The tax applies in addition to any estate or gift tax otherwise applicable to the same transfer.

The Three Types of GST Transfers

Three categories of transfer can produce GST tax:

1. **Direct skips.** Transfers directly to a person two or more generations below the transferor — typically a grandchild. The GST tax is computed and paid at the time of transfer (by the transferor, in the case of a gift, or by the estate, in the case of a bequest).

2. **Taxable distributions.** Distributions from a trust to a person two or more generations below the transferor (a skip person). GST tax is paid by the recipient.
3. **Taxable terminations.** The termination of an interest in a trust where, after the termination, only skip persons hold interests in the trust. GST tax is paid by the trustee.

GST Exemption

Each individual has a GST exemption that can be allocated to particular transfers. The exemption is set at the same dollar level as the federal estate-tax exemption and is indexed the same way. Portability does not apply to GST — the unused exemption of one spouse is not available to the surviving spouse. Each spouse's GST exemption must be used during life or at death; unused exemption is lost.

Allocation of GST exemption is reported on Form 706 (at death) or Form 709 (during life). Default allocation rules apply when no affirmative allocation is made; the default rules can be unfavorable, which is why affirmative allocation is often preferred. Counsel specializing in transfer tax should handle GST allocations.

The Predeceased Parent Exception

If the transferor's child has predeceased the transferor at the time of a transfer to that child's descendants, the descendants are not treated as skip persons for GST purposes. The transfer is treated as if it had gone to the deceased child, who would not have been a skip person. This exception applies to lineal descendants (grandchildren, great-grandchildren) where their intervening parent is dead at the time of transfer.

Common GST Traps

- Trusts established for grandchildren without timely allocation of GST exemption.
- Outright bequests to grandchildren when the parent is still alive (a direct skip; uses GST exemption).
- Older trusts that have continued past the original beneficiary's death — taxable terminations may apply.
- Failure to elect out of the automatic-allocation rules where appropriate.
- Married couples failing to use both spouses' GST exemptions through trust structures.

Practical Implications

GST tax is technical enough that families with potential exposure should engage specialist counsel rather than relying on general estate-planning attorneys. The cost of specialist guidance is modest relative to the potential 40% federal tax on mishandled transfers. For families without potential exposure (most American families), the GST tax is a non-issue.

APPENDIX N

Charitable Planning Structures

Charitable transfers are entirely outside the federal transfer-tax system — the unlimited charitable deduction applies for both estate-tax purposes (IRC §2055) and gift-tax purposes (IRC §2522). For families with charitable inclinations, a range of structures permits philanthropic transfers in tax-efficient ways.

Outright Charitable Bequests

The simplest structure: a bequest under the will or trust directing assets to a qualified charity. The bequest is fully deductible for estate-tax purposes. No tax. The charity receives the asset directly.

For testators with appreciated assets, charitable bequests are particularly efficient: the asset receives a stepped-up basis in the hands of the deceased's estate (under §1014), avoiding any capital-gains tax that would have applied if the asset had been sold during life. The charity can then sell the asset tax-free (as a §501(c)(3) organization). The full appreciated value reaches charity.

Charitable Remainder Trusts

A charitable remainder trust (CRT) provides income to named non-charitable beneficiaries (often the donor or donor's family) for a term of years or for life, with the remainder passing to a charity at the end of the term. The donor receives an immediate income-tax deduction for the present value of the eventual charitable remainder; the trust assets are removed from the donor's estate.

Two principal variants exist:

- Charitable Remainder Annuity Trust (CRAT) — pays a fixed dollar amount annually to non-charitable beneficiaries.
- Charitable Remainder Unitrust (CRUT) — pays a fixed percentage of the trust's value annually, recomputed each year.

CRTs are particularly useful for highly appreciated assets (typically marketable securities or real property). The trust can sell the appreciated asset without capital-gains tax (as a tax-exempt entity), reinvest the proceeds, and pay income to the donor over time.

Charitable Lead Trusts

A charitable lead trust (CLT) is the mirror image of a CRT. The trust pays a fixed amount to a charity for a term of years, with the remainder passing to non-charitable beneficiaries (often the donor's children or grandchildren) at the end of the term. The donor receives a present-value gift-tax deduction for the charitable interest. CLTs are particularly useful in low-interest-rate environments because the present-value computation favors the charitable interest at lower rates.

Donor-Advised Funds

A donor-advised fund (DAF) is an account at a sponsoring charity (community foundation or commercial sponsor) to which the donor contributes assets, receives an immediate income-tax deduction, and then advises the sponsor on the timing and recipients of grants from the DAF. The structure permits bunched charitable giving (combining several years of contributions into one for deduction purposes) and ongoing charitable engagement without operating a private foundation.

Private Foundations

A private foundation is a separate non-profit organization, typically funded and governed by a single family or individual. Foundations offer the greatest flexibility and family engagement but carry operational complexity (annual filing requirements, minimum-distribution rules, prohibited-transaction rules, excise taxes). Private foundations are usually appropriate only for substantial charitable commitments and families who want active multi-generational philanthropic engagement.

Choosing Among the Structures

The right charitable structure depends on the family's goals and financial circumstances. As a rough guide:

- Outright bequests — for donors with simple intentions and no need for income from the assets.
- DAFs — for donors who want flexibility, simplicity, and ongoing engagement without operating a foundation.
- CRTs — for donors with highly appreciated assets who want income during life and a charitable remainder.
- CLTs — for donors who want charitable benefit now and family transfer later (effective in low-rate environments).
- Private foundations — for substantial commitments and families who want active multi-generational philanthropy.

Each structure has technical requirements that exceed this appendix. Specialist counsel is essential for any implementation.

A FINAL WORD

On Tax Law, Care, and the Quiet Years Before

◆

You have come to the end of this volume. You have read, perhaps, more about estate taxes than you ever expected to need to know.

And yet what this book has been describing, in its own structured way, is something quieter and larger than estate tax itself.

It has been describing the act of taking care.

The transfer-tax system exists because someone, at some point in the long history of American public finance, decided that the transfer of large accumulations of wealth between generations deserved a structured treatment. Every exemption ever indexed, every inclusion rule ever drafted, every basis-step-up ever applied is at its root part of the same coordinated effort: to allow most families to transfer what they have built without tax friction, while imposing a structured cost on the largest concentrations of wealth.

That structured cost is what most of this book has been about. But the deeper subject is the same one that has anchored each of the four volumes of The Complete Estate & Property Planning

Series.

You have learned what estate taxes are, what they are not, why they exist, what gets counted, how the exemption works, why timing matters more than amounts, how gift taxes connect to estate taxes, what the basis-step-up does, when capital gains apply, and the recurring patterns of surprise. What you do now with that knowledge — for yourself, for your family, for the people who will eventually inherit what you leave behind — is the real subject of this book.

Compute your gross estate honestly. Know your state-level exposure. Implement the structures that move appreciable assets out of the estate well before they are needed. Preserve the basis-step-up for everything else. Update your plan when life changes. Engage your CPA and counsel. Have the conversations the family has been postponing.

"A plan is not made in the moment of crisis. It is made in the quiet years before the crisis, and tested — silently, invisibly — every day thereafter. The legacy worth leaving is the one your loved ones never have to wonder about."

And so the four-volume series ends where each book began — with the same sentence that we hope you will carry with you, and pass forward, long after you have closed these pages:

"Estate planning is not paperwork. It is the form love takes when it has to outlast the person who felt it."

Take care of yours.

— AVOY Publishing

Spring 2026

Made in the USA
Coppell, TX
04 November 2026

11207676R00154